Founding Families of

PITTSBURGH

Founding Families

OF PITTSBURGH

THE EVOLUTION
OF A REGIONAL ELITE
1760 – 1910

Joseph F. Rishel

UNIVERSITY OF PITTSBURGH PRESS

Published by the University of Pittsburgh Press, Pittsburgh, Pa. 15260
Copyright © 1990 University of Pittsburgh Press
Baker & Taylor International, London
Manufactured in the United States of America

Library of Congress Cataloging-in-Publication Data

Rishel, Joseph Francis, 1945–
    Founding families of Pittsburgh : the evolution of a regional
elite, 1760–1910 / Joseph F. Rishel.
        p. cm.
    Includes bibliographical references.
    ISBN 0-8229-3633-X
    1. Elite (Social sciences)—Pennsylvania—Pittsburgh—Longitudinal
studies. 2. Elite (Social sciences)—Pennsylvania—Pittsburgh—
History—19th century. I. Title.
HN80.P6R57   1990
305.5′52′0974886—dc20   89-39006
                                                                  CIP

For Helen

CONTENTS

PREFACE

For some time now historians have approached history and the writing of history more systematically than their predecessors did. Reliance on private papers, newspapers, and other such sources as the raw material of writing history has been supplanted, or at least supplemented, by federal censuses, city directories, election returns, and other compilations by which heads are counted and lives delineated. Much of this history has been aimed at uncovering the heretofore unknown lives of the common person. Although these people were unlikely to have kept a diary or amassed any relevant body of papers, it was still possible to find out much about their lives.

This type of research inevitably involves quantitative analysis. Historians found themselves talking numbers as they related life histories, or as was more commonly the case, generalized life cycles. The problems faced by Frank L. Owsley in his 1949 study of everyday people in the antebellum South have been addressed by each subsequent generation of historians. The difficulty lies in presenting a historically accurate picture of the times while balancing the need for detailed information with the "finite range of man's life and the finite qualities of the reader's patience with and interest in statistics."[1] The problem of presenting these statistics in an interesting and meaningful way—exceeded only by the extreme tedium experienced by the researcher in collecting them—is great to be sure, but not insurmountable.

Such studies furnish insight into the larger trends that shape history. Movements that were vaguely and often inaccurately described in anecdotal historical records can be properly assessed for their strength and significance. Even the study of individual lives acquires greater meaning when considered in the frame of reference provided by quantitative studies.

These studies need not be restricted to the lower or middle classes of society. The vast majority of the upper class has not deposited personal papers in archives publicly available to researchers. Those papers of families or individuals that are extant are so varied in composition as to render any uniform arrangement of data nearly impossible.

The art of collecting data on the lives of numerous individuals and making a single portrait of the group has recently been given the rather impressive name of *prosopography*. This word is derived from the Greek *prosopopoiia* (to make a person), hence prosopography is the activity of producing a collection of biographies. This study of the founding families of Allegheny County will employ the techniques of prosopography and will frequently express the findings statistically. Since the quantitative findings are often supported by individual case histories, it is hoped that neither the readers' patience nor interest will be strained.

ACKNOWLEDGMENTS

The writing of this book owes much to a great many people. I should like to thank Walter S. Glazer who originally directed this research and to whom part of the conceptual framework must be credited. Van Beck Hall, a scholar of considerable merit as well as a good friend, has been an excellent critic. His help in creating a sharper focus for many ideas contained herein cannot be repaid. My thanks also go to Burton W. Folsom, whose interest in social mobility is well known. We spent many hours discussing that subject. My manuscript also received considerable critical review from my wife, Helen Krebs Rishel. Constructive criticism was also given by Samuel P. Hays and Robert W. Doherty.

The collection of data for this study involved an expenditure of time and effort the likes of which I shall never, in my right mind, undertake again. A host of libraries and archives was used on a trip that took me across the United States in an effort to track down elusive migrants. In Pittsburgh, the Pennsylvania Division of Carnegie Public Library was a resource of enormous value. The librarians there were always helpful and no amount of praise could be too much. It was the Pennsylvania Division with which Frank W. Powelson entrusted the care and preservation of his "Founding Families of Allegheny County." Since my own study is so dependent on Powelson's work, in whose honor it is named, I offer a very special thanks. Would that he had lived to see this book published. I also made extensive use of the library of the Historical Society of Western Pennsylvania. Its collection of family histories and genealogies was invaluable. Frank Zabrosky, Curator of the Archives of Industrial Society at the University of Pittsburgh, was of great assistance, not only by helping me to exploit his own collection, but by suggesting other sources for me to use. Without the help of all of these, this study would not have been possible.

Finally, I would like to thank Duquesne University for the support it gave in the preparation of this book.

Founding Families of

PITTSBURGH

I

The Historical Framework

T HIS IS a study of individuals and of families. It is a collective biographical, or prosopographical, analysis of twenty of the "founding families" of Pittsburgh and Allegheny County, Pennsylvania. It traces the evolution of these families from their founders through successive generations, beginning in the late revolutionary period and ending in the early twentieth century. The purpose of the study is to describe the internal composition of this group of families to determine the degree to which they formed a clearly defined, coherent upper class, and the extent to which they were able to maintain their status over time. The study therefore examines first, the social character and composition of the founding families; second, their position within the larger society; and third, the career patterns of family members.

Although the study is concerned with the status of founding family members within their own socioeconomic circles, it is also rooted in the history and development of Allegheny County itself. The resources and opportunities of the region shaped and directed the destinies of these families. They changed and were themselves changed by their physical, economic, and cultural milieu. Many of them chose to leave the area permanently. An important aspect of this study is that it traces those outmigrants and contrasts them with those relatives who maintained their roots and connections in Allegheny County.

Although initially indistinguishable as a group from the larger population in terms of their social and cultural characteristics, by the end of the nineteenth century the majority of the founding families had formed a distinct group easily distinguishable from the rest of the population. As we shall see, they began the 1800s as a heterogeneous group, socially distinct from one another. But by the end of the century their descendants, or more accurately, those who had utilized their advantages most successfully, had formed an identifiable and homogeneous upper class. In tracing the careers of the family founders and their descendants, the social mechanisms that they employed in order to achieve and maintain elite status will be examined. These mechanisms relied on the assistance of associates and other family members, since one seldom enters the ranks of the elite merely on one's own efforts and accomplishments. One must first be launched from a strategic position from which the family contacts and associations with successful individuals can be employed. The launch which the individual receives has been called the "main chance," "takeoff," or even a "break," all implying a sudden departure from a previous, less desirable position on the socioeconomic scale.[1] Once this "main chance" is successfully negotiated, the rising individual realizes what I call the "accumulation of advantages" (a theme carried throughout this book), a combination of achievement, opportunity, and the psychological readiness to promote oneself to even higher levels.

Most of the rich who are descended from wealthy ancestors were born with the accumulation of advantages already firmly established; the main chance had already been made for them. It should be noted, however, that while wealth is certainly an important element in the attainment of elite status, one's position is not measured simply in dollars and cents. The accumulation of advantages manifests itself in many ways: socially, educationally, in mate selection, and so forth, not solely in the economic sphere.

Nor does the accumulation of advantages operate to the

same degree for all who have realized the main chance; rather, it yields its benefits in proportion to one's position within the socioeconomic order. As C. Wright Mills has said, "Opportunity is limited by [one's] position within the stratification of the society."[2] The accumulation of advantages, therefore, determines how much of society's benefits are accessible: one's ascent in this scale means that society will offer additional benefits.[3]

Once the ascent has been realized, the accumulation of advantages performs a maintenance function, that is, it prevents downward social mobility. Since the major portion of this study is concerned with those generations following the family founders, the ability of the accumulation of advantages to prevent downward mobility is of great importance. From this some speculations concerning the nature of American society may be ventured.

Popular American beliefs have traditionally compared American society to a European counterpart. Without an aristocratic inheritance by which classes may be defined, entrance into the American elite is theoretically possible for anyone with the opportunity, ambition, and good fortune to make enough money. This openness to penetration from below, based on achievement, has resulted in popular suppositions of American equality. But equality does not dictate equal chances of success—the cards are decidedly stacked in favor of some. Once success is achieved, the rewards of success are enjoyed by succeeding generations. The offspring of the successful are given a push on the road to success that is not granted to the lowly. Thus success for some is achieved partially through the efforts of others.

Achievement results in an individual becoming a member of the elite. The term *elite* therefore refers to occupational success. A member of the elite is functionally (occupationally) prominent, but not necessarily extremely wealthy or included in the social upper class. Families who have continued to be occupationally prominent often find acceptance into the social upper class in later generations.

America's supposedly open society, as opposed to Europe's supposedly closed one, permits the individual either to fall from a high position or rise from a low one. Since class is based upon achievement in America, not upon nobility, class status can be lost as well as gained. In reality, the upward and downward mobility of succeeding generations serves as an indicator of the openness of the class structure as well as the effectiveness of the accumulation of advantages in maintaining one's status against fresh competitors.

The openness and fluidity of American society must be considered in "the long run," that is, the period extending beyond the first generation which achieved, was rewarded, and became elite. Clearly America does reward achievement; the important consideration for the historian is the character and composition of succeeding generations and their relationship to the rest of society. If there is no downward social mobility, then American society is closed and approximates popular notions of European society. If, in the long run, there is downward social mobility from elite status in the same amount and extent as exists in the rest of society, then the society is open. If, in the long run, there is some downward social mobility from elite status but not to the amount and extent as exists in the rest of society, then there is a class structure that has continuity and denies equal opportunity to achieve to the more ambitious but less privileged. This elite, that is, the rewarded group, by virtue of reward, occupies an elevated position creating inequality of condition but not necessarily inequality of opportunity. Over time it becomes an upper class.

In order to establish the degree of openness of the upper class, whether inclusion is based on achievement or heredity, one must study both the original elite and subsequent generations. This is a major part of this study. More specifically, my object is to examine the extent to which the accumulation of advantages was a factor in preventing downward social mobility in the long run. This process must be observed in as broad a context as possible, in the group's internal development and in its interaction with the rest of society. The findings should contribute to our understanding of American society.

There are essentially two tests that can be performed to determine the degree to which the class structure is open or closed. The first measures the extent to which those born below a given class—in this study, the upper class—are able to move up and be accepted into that class. The second measures the extent to which those born in a given class—in this study, again, the upper class—are maintained there, presumably by the accumulation of advantages, or fall from it. To date, the study of upward mobility has attracted the interests of social scientists far more than downward mobility.

But social mobility has been both upward and downward; those who study upward mobility exclusively may well be misled in their interpretation of society. This is especially true of the United States which, historically, has undergone rapid growth not only in its population, economy, and territory, but also in technology. Many menial, low-status occupations were eliminated and skilled, higher-status occupations were created, contributing to an uneven but universal rise in the standard of living and an upward shift in the class structure. In view of the enormous increase of opportunity at the top, it is small wonder that social scientists have found that a significant proportion of the population was able to raise its social status and that the upper class was open to penetration from below. Consequent to this dramatically increasing number of positions at the top, some individuals would inevitably rise to fill them. However, it is not necessary for those individuals already at the top to be displaced. If the upper class were closed to downward mobility, it would merely slow the rate of rising individuals. If individuals who have achieved upper-class status or have been born to it can decline, the society is fluid. It is possible that in a historical study of American society, downward mobility is the more reliable of the two indicators if any judgment is to be made concerning its openness.[4]

The large number of studies of the elite has failed to reach any real consensus on the question of the openness of American society. Despite the use of the latest social science techniques, historians have arrived at contradictory conclusions concerning upward or downward social mobility. In their efforts to reach accurate conclusions, historians have compiled mountains of information from censuses, city directories, wills, county histories, and biographical encyclopedias as well as from the more traditional sources such as diaries, newspapers, personal correspondence, and family biographies.[5]

Probably the classic quantitative historical study of the upper class remains the pioneering work, *Philadelphia Gentlemen: The Making of a National Upper Class,* by E. Digby Baltzell. Baltzell uses a sociologist's functional analysis to describe the upper class in Philadelphia. His sample forms a part of what he calls an American business aristocracy of colonial stock and Protestant affiliation. Baltzell presents a multidimensional view as he examines their family backgrounds as far back in American history as the data permit, and their changing "neighborhood" relationships, religious affiliations, educational practices, and club memberships. He also analyzes their public roles and those of their families in politics, journalism, the professions, letters, art, and philanthropy.[6]

Although the subtitle implies a historical approach, only three of the fifteen chapters are historical in nature. Of the three, only "Neighborhood and Class Structure" develops the theme historically, describing upper-class neighborhoods and geographically plotting their locations and movements from the colonial era to 1940. The other two chapters are concerned with the founding of particular families in the period immediately preceding or immediately following the Civil War. Baltzell then compares these earlier families with the upper class of 1940. There is, however, no continuum of treatment through the intervening generations. The fact that elite families of the pre– and post–Civil War periods have a descendant who was in *Who's Who in America* and the *Social Register* in 1940 should not be surprising; surely of all the descendants of the family founders, some should be able to "maintain" themselves.[7]

The treatment of the family founders as compared to the 1940 upper class is ahistorical. Baltzell takes the elite group of the upper class from the *Social Register* in 1940 and demonstrates that they had well-established ancestors before 1900 (many before 1865). To argue backward, that because the upper class in 1940 had upper-class roots before 1900 it must be a coherent, self-sustaining elite, does not necessarily prove the thesis of upper-class continuity. Baltzell is dealing only with a small, select portion of the descendants of the nineteenth-century elite who maintained their position through 1940. The argument becomes a self-fulfilling one. What he proves is that these individuals who were in the upper class in 1940 had this advantage. In order to establish whether there is a strong line of continuity and cohesion within the upper class over generations it is necessary to argue progressively, not retrogressively, by taking an upper-class group at the beginning, and determining whether its descendants were able to maintain their favorable position. In this way one can establish a historically valid argument for Baltzell's thesis: that there has always been an elite, and that its composition over generations has remained stable.

Though Baltzell purports to demonstrate the development of a nationwide upper class, the entirety of his group are Philadelphia residents in 1940. Since the group has meaning only in a particular locality, anyone who migrates is "lost" from the group and is not considered, even though the author is ostensibly concerned with the development of a national, not a local, upper class. The group has a logic and a meaning only in Philadelphia.[8]

In contrast to Baltzell, this study of the founding families of Allegheny County is chronologically progressive in tracing succeeding generations. It also attempts to follow all descendants of the family founders, whether they stayed in Allegheny County or migrated from it. The multidimensional view used so successfully by Baltzell is in this study not confined to a single point in time. Rather it is applied consistently over the entirety of the period. The considerations of historical development and geographic mobility add important dimensions to the study of the founding families of Allegheny County.

My approach is similar to Baltzell's in its multidimensional treatment of individuals, that is, in viewing them in terms of occupation, religious affiliation, education, and so on. We differ, however, in both the spatial and time dimension; Baltzell's main thrust is the individual in a particular time, 1940, and a particular place, Philadelphia. My study treats individuals over an extended period of time and, once the group is established in Allegheny County by 1820, follows them wherever they go.

Since almost all social mobility studies are concerned with a particular area, those who leave are simply categorized as "lost," or largely unsubstantiated conjectures are made concerning their fate. As Stuart Mack Blumin admits, rates of mobility within a given city "cannot be generalized to the nation at large until more is known about the relationship between vertical mobility and migration."[9] It is here that a study of the founding families of Allegheny County can make a major contribution. To the extent that it is possible, those who do leave are followed.

While Baltzell finds elite antecedents to the Philadelphia upper class in 1940, he gives no indication of the number of descendants who had lost elite status. Others have studied the rates of downward mobility using quantitative analysis. Their findings differ markedly over a broad spectrum with respect to time and place and have resulted in divergent interpretations concerning the degree of openness of American society. These historians can be broadly defined by two opposing schools of thought: those who find relatively little downward mobility, inferring a closed society; and those who find significantly higher rates of downward mobility and thus infer a more open society.

Prominent among those whose findings support elite continuity, with little downward mobility, is Edward Pessen. Concerning antebellum society in New York City, Philadelphia, Brooklyn, and Boston, he claims that with few exceptions the rich inherited and held onto their wealth and connections. Pessen did find continuity among elite families, but he did not include all descendants in these families, only the successful.[10] All of the offspring were followed in Lee Benson's study of the Philadelphia economic elite of the 1800s. This approach revealed a fluid society with much upward and downward mobility.[11] Frederick C. Jaher found in his study of the "upper strata" in Boston, New York, Charleston, Chicago, and Los Angeles that the degrees of continuity "were defined by local historical circumstances." The Boston and Charleston elite experienced a high degree of persistence, while in the dynamic economy of New York City, successive waves of new elites changed the character and composition of that city's upper class. Chicago's burgeoning population also brought a newly rich elite which attempted to reproduce the social stability of older eastern cities. In Los Angeles, however, the upper class never achieved stability, having been overwhelmed by hordes of movie stars and motion picture tycoons. Jaher attempts to view the upper strata as a whole over time, including each new economic elite.[12]

The different conclusions derived from these studies of upper-class continuity are largely dependent upon whether or not the researcher has a geographical focus, which determines whether he or she is concerned with the persistence of individual families or upper-class structure. This study of Allegheny County's founding families focuses on the continuity of the original elite families, regardless of the composition of the entire upper class. Indeed, in succeeding generations following the original family founders, geographical placement in Allegheny County is no longer of primary importance. Thus, the total composition of the upper class in Allegheny County is not significant in this study of family persistence.

In most studies, the findings are, in large part, predetermined by the sampling techniques employed. An example of this is William Miller's analysis of the social origins of America's corporate elite of 1910. Although he finds that 80 percent of the corporate presidents and board chairmen studied had fathers who were businessmen or professionals, his selection of men in the older, less dynamic enterprises, such as textiles and railroads, predisposed the findings to reveal a higher degree of continuity.[13] Because my study is not wedded to any occupational group, the family founders represent a wide spectrum of businesses and professions.

John Ingham's study of the iron and steel elite focuses on a particular industry in six cities. Due to the fact that he studied this industry in a period of enormous technological change and growth, he discovered a high degree of continuity as family members were pulled into the corporate network. His study included a wide range of considerations: it avoided a narrow geographical focus by researching six different cities, it followed all descendants, and it was multidimensional in terms of the criteria employed in determining success.[14]

Given the methodology employed by Ingham, it is surprising that his findings are sharply in conflict with those of Burton Folsom, who happened to study one of the same cities in the same time period.[15] Whereas Ingham's study of Bethlehem, Pennsylvania, in the late nineteenth and early twentieth centuries revealed a high degree of corporate continuity, Folsom found few successful sons succeeding successful fathers. The difference in their conclusions may be explained by their definitions of success. Ingham pronounced the sons successful if they were elevated to the board of their respective corporations; Folsom insisted that they retain those positions of responsibility through a period of corporate mergers in order to be deemed successful.

In considering the findings of Ingham and Folsom in their studies of Bethlehem, there appears to be an explanation for the differing conclusions reached by historians studying downward mobility other than just differences in time and place. The selection of the elite and the criteria imposed in deciding what constitutes downward mobility play a vital role.

The particular character of this elite is also of immense importance. For Folsom's Scranton elite, there was virtually no room for upward mobility, only downward mobility, as his group was at the very pinnacle of wealth and power. Since they were an industrial elite in a time of extremely rapid technological change, it was necessary for their children to advance quickly to preserve their places in the socioeconomic order. By contrast, the founding families of Allegheny County, originating in a preindustrial elite, had at least some room to rise even within elite circles. Moreover, with their fortunes not resting solely on continued technological innovation, their positions may have been less precarious although they were even less able to rest on the achievements of the family founders. Stability, family connections, and caution, all of which ultimately contributed to the decline of Folsom's Scranton elite, could be used to advantage by the founding families of Allegheny County.

II

Discovering the Founding Families

A NY QUANTITATIVE STUDY of an elite is dependent upon reliable sources for determining who actually belongs to that group.[1] Identifying these individuals in a preindustrial society without an aristocracy presents special problems not confronted by those studying elites in a later period with more formalized systems of identification. Still, there are a variety of sources available, albeit limited in number: lists that reveal occupation, such as tax rolls and city directories; records of governmental officeholders; and records of directors of charitable or civic organizations, business associations, or other groups that the researcher has identified as truly elite in makeup. These sources tend to be unidimensional in that occupational descriptions are too loosely defined or they embrace only one aspect of an individual's career.

In preparing this study I was fortunately able to use the "Founding Families of Allegheny County," by Frank W. Powelson, a compilation that he describes as "a record of some of the prominent families of the city of Pittsburgh."[2] His five-volume work gives genealogies of 129 eminent pre–Civil War families of Pittsburgh and Allegheny County and traces their descendants into the twentieth century. He based his work on wills filed with the Register of Wills of Allegheny County, Pennsylvania, 1789–1867, and supplemented this information with a variety of other publicly available sources. Powelson used four criteria for determining which families would be included in his index. First, the family must have arrived in Allegheny County before 1860. Second, it must have filed a will prior to 1868. Third, the family founder must have achieved such prominence that his name appears in one or more of the various published lists of notable people. Fourth, the family founder was a Freemason.[3]

Among the earliest sources that substantiate Powelson's index as being truly an elite index is "Prominent Citizens of Pittsburgh, Pennsylvania," published as a part of the *Honest Man's Almanac* in 1812.[4] Of the 148 people listed, 31 percent are also in Powelson's index. However, the almanac included only city residents—Powelson treated all of Allegheny County—and was published long before Powelson's 1860 cutoff date. Only eleven of the twenty families in the sample group used for this study were city residents by 1812; nine of them appear in the almanac. (The two not listed were undeniably socially prominent as well as wealthy, but the author of the almanac stated that the list was incomplete.)

From the 129 families in Powelson's index, I selected a sample of 20 families. The selection was not entirely random, however. Only 77 of the 129 families were present in 1820, the year I chose as the cutoff date for my study. A further 16 families were excluded because Powelson gave no genealogies, only lists of names and dates. Twenty-two families were excluded because their surnames were too common, often making identification of a specific individual difficult or impossible when using public sources. From the 39 remaining names, 20 were randomly selected for study.

The 20 families include a total of 1,006 individuals, from the family founder to the last person born in the time frame of this study. Typically, but dependent upon the arrival of the family founder in Allegheny County, this period embraces four generations. As a rule, all those born prior to 1880 were included in the sample.[5]

Although the history of the founding families is really a continuum of overlapping generations, for purposes of comparison and analysis it is appropriate to divide the time frame into three periods which identify stages of growth in Pittsburgh as well as in the United States. These are referred to in this study as the 1820 period, the 1860 period, and the 1900 period. The 1820 period, by far the longest, includes those individuals whose adult lives fell largely or entirely within a preindustrial era. The year 1820 marked the latest allowable date for the arrival of a family founder in Allegheny County, but the span encompassed by the 1820 period begins with the arrival of the first family founder in 1760 and ends about 1840. The 1860 period was largely a transitional one, economically as well as socially. It generally encompasses individuals whose adult lives fell between the years 1840 to 1880. The 1900 period is seen in this study as the final stage in the development of the founding families, reflecting a more nationally structured upper class beginning about 1880. The period continues to approximately 1910 in order to include the careers of the last born in the final generation studied.

The entire sample is divided into "core" and "non-core" group members. The slightly smaller core group, numbering 468, or 47 percent of the total, is composed of the originally selected family founders and their descendants who retain the surname. All males who married into the core group, and their children, compose the non-core group, numbering 538 (53 percent). All descendants having the surname of the original family founder are included in the study and are designated core group members. Founding family daughters who marry and thus acquire a new surname are considered non-core, as are their husbands and children. This study follows the children of such marriages (including daughters), but not the grandchildren. This decision was made to prevent too great a dilution of the family influence and to retain the original 20 family surnames as the focus of this study. Figure 1 demonstrates which individuals were included in a hypothetical family through four generations. It also shows how the non-core surnames naturally increase at a rate exceeding that of the core. All the individuals are shown as having married and all such marriages having one son and one daughter.

Powelson's index was intended to be a genealogy, and

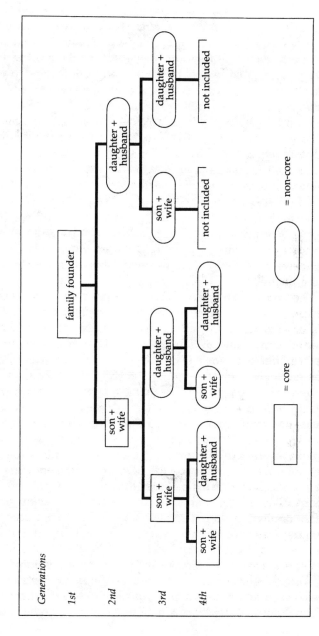

FIGURE 1. Hypothetical Genealogy Showing Core and Non-Core Groups

although giving such vital facts as dates of birth and death, names of parents, children, and spouses, it almost never contains any other information. Although family descent was clearly established, a host of other sources were used to provide the multidimensional view of individual careers which a study of this sort necessitates. Some remarks must be made regarding the nature of these sources as well as their reliability. In attempting a collective biography, the researcher is subject to much the same difficulties as are encountered by the traditional historian. Because he or she must rely upon family histories and biographical encyclopedias that are usually privately published, the researcher must consider the accuracy of the information they contain.

The biographical encyclopedias that flourished in the late nineteenth and early twentieth centuries were published for profit and typically required payment from those who wished to be included (see Bibliography of Biographical sources). Families which were once prominent but had moved away, died out, or sharply declined in economic status were omitted by publishers from the pantheon of illustrious families. Omitted too were families which, out of a kind of inverse snobbery and confidence in their own social status, refused to pay in order to be included.

Because they were sold by subscription, these encyclopedias came to be known as "puff books": they had to "puff up" or exaggerate the fame and even the occupational importance of their subjects. Some have alleged that a fantasy world was created wherein tellers were called bankers, but this has not generally been found to be the case. Although they are replete with laudatory comments, the researcher can readily discard these along with the typical closing sentence of the article drenching the subject with praise as being "truly an upright Christian man, a source of inspiration to all who know him."

Far more subtle distortions did occur, however. John Boucher, in his genealogy of the Dilworth family, changed the name of the firm of Colart and Dilworth to the more flattering Dilworth and Colart.[6] If this may be considered trivial, some biographical encyclopedias were willing to go to far greater lengths in bending the truth. Of Maj. Gen. James Scott Negley's military career, the *Biographical Encyclopedia* states in noncommital language, "He participated prominently in the battle of Chickamauga." Fleming's *History of Pittsburgh and Environs* went considerably further: "At Chickamauga, Rossville and Chattanooga his services make for him, indeed, a proud record." But the impeccable and nonsubscriptive *Dictionary of American Biography* gave quite a different acccount. "[At] Chickamauga along with other commanders on the right wing of the Union line, he was swept back from the battlefield." In addition, the *DAB* revealed that General Negley was relieved of his command and court-martialed for cowardice and desertion, hardly "a proud record" despite the fact that he was later acquitted of the charges.[7]

Occasionally the subscribers attached as great an importance to the length of the family's genealogy as to its content. In the *Encyclopedia of Pennsylvania Biography*, Jane Kennedy Nimick traced her ancestors prior to the second century A.D.[8] Not to be outdone, and straining the credulity of the reader to the breaking point, Mrs. Emma Fahnestock O'Leary traced her pedigree to Adam.[9]

While admittedly they impugn the integrity of the rest of the text, the above shortcomings, including the Negley example, do not seriously affect the data. The fact that Negley attained the rank of general is of greater significance than the success of a single military conflict. The researcher must be alert, however, for misrepresentations that damage the reliability of the data. The biographer of John S. Dilworth, for example, states that he "was educated in the private schools of Mount Washington." From another source it was learned that his father had, at his own expense, provided a teacher and built a one-room school which the Dilworth children attended along with some neighborhood children.[10] Certainly this does not fit the popular conception of a private school in 1908, the year when the biography was written. This was a deliberate attempt to deceive rather than enlighten the reader.

If the biographical encyclopedias deserve censure for such

distortions, the family genealogies are guilty of a different set of transgressions. Apart from the most serious one, that of incomplete data, they are at times unclear. The author's familiarity with the people mentioned may result in confusion for the reader, who does not know the family relationships. "On the death of Elizabeth, Mary returned to Pittsburgh where she lived with my mother and later in the country at my Uncle John's home."[11] This style characterized several of the genealogies which ranged from good and informative to poor and uninformative. Apart from the genealogies provided by Powelson's index, family histories have been written about only twelve of the twenty families.

Despite these shortcomings, much of the data about the founding families was obtained from the biographical encyclopedias and family genealogies. For two reasons I believe that the distortions did not affect my observations or conclusions about the history of the families. First, the material I collected was of a basic nature (place of birth, date of birth, religion, and so on) and was unconcerned that the subject was "a source of inspiration." The author would have had little reason to misrepresent such elementary statistics. Second, in an effort to find additional information, I used as many sources as possible for each person, thus in effect cross-checking and verifying the facts.

The information on each individual was coded and then analyzed using SPSS (Statistical Package for the Social Sciences). The categories used were:

> Core or non-core
> Sex
> Year born
> Year died
> Generation number
> Time period: 1820, 1860, 1900
> Where born
> Where died
> Nationality
> Religion
> Church official?

Education
Spouse
Year married
Where married
Spouse's father's occupation
Married a relative?
Number of children
Residence 1800–1910 (decennially)
Occupation(s) (in chronological order up to 6)
Greatest number of jobs held concurrently
Family firm employment code
Upper-class club?
Trusteeship?
Political party

For several variables the amount of data is meager and the results are less significant statistically. The conventional level of statistical significance is fairly strict. For the findings to be accepted as reliable, the probability of the data occurring by accident must be less than one chance in twenty.[12] The statistical data presented by historians often fail to pass this test because the total cross-tabulated relationships frequently exceed the number allowable given the quantity of cases used. This, however, is one hazard in research of this nature; the alternatives are to say nothing at all about nineteenth-century society or to abandon all quantitative study and rely solely upon traditional literature. In this study, every effort has been made to satisfy the requirements of statistical significance and to assure reliable results. In categories where data was insufficient to meet these requirements, political party affiliation, for example, definitive statements are not ventured.

III

The Family Founders

The Pittsburgh Region

ALLEGHENY COUNTY is a portion of a great uneven plateau that slopes westward about one hundred fifty miles from the Appalachian Mountains. The Appalachians, seven hundred miles in length, almost one hundred miles wide, and frequently exceeding three thousand feet in height, presented a formidable barrier in preindustrial times. Chestnut Ridge, the westernmost of the ridges, is only thirty-four miles from Pittsburgh, the county seat. In addition to significantly retarding migration, transportation, and communication, these mountains "prevented an easy exchange of ideas between the people of the East and those to the west of the mountains."[1] Perhaps of even greater importance is the fact that the ranges "localized the transmontane pioneers and engendered a cultural and political ideology which became manifest in their political behavior."[2]

While the mountains separated the area from the East, the northern portion of the plateau was united by the Allegheny and Monongahela river systems, which spread throughout Western Pennsylvania and, converging at Pittsburgh, "tended to point the commerce and the interest of the rural settlers in that direction."[3] At Pittsburgh, these rivers form the Ohio, a part of the Mississippi system and, since the times of the

22

earliest explorations, the nation's main artery to the interior lowland and to the South. In the preindustrial period, the topography of the area focused the energies and interests of Pittsburghers and the founding families of Allegheny County on the West and South rather than on the East.

The fertility of the soil, supplemented by appropriate rainfall and a temperate climate, supported a comparatively dense agricultural population. For this reason, the region's chief exports in the eighteenth and early nineteenth centuries were products of the soil, especially grain and its derivatives. The first heavy influx of settlers occurred after the collapse of Pontiac's conspiracy at the Battle of Bushy Run in 1763. A royal proclamation of that year forbidding settlement west of the mountains proved ineffectual in stemming the migration.

The existence of a large rural population and the presence of Fort Pitt, with the safety it afforded, led to the growth of an urban community to serve the region. Founded in 1758 and destined to be the focal point of the upper Ohio Valley, Pittsburgh had already become a town of 130 families by 1792. Including the military, this must have raised Pittsburgh's population to well over one thousand, far larger than any potential competitor in the region. Its numerical superiority and economic importance increased with the passing of each decade.

The very mountains that isolated the area from the East partly determined the nature of the county's economic development. Local merchants were denied full participation in the lucrative import-export trade that was building vast family fortunes in eastern coastal cities even before the War of 1812. Pittsburgh manufacturers, however, benefited from the lack of foreign competition for their products. Geographically protected from the cheaper goods produced by Great Britain's industrial revolution, Pittsburgh's entrepreneurs were nonetheless able to borrow British technology. In the opening decades of the nineteenth century this generated a number of vigorous infant industries.

Although the rivers tended to direct the area's trade to New Orleans and the South, the economic elite of Allegheny

County was unable to imitate its southern counterparts. Pittsburgh did not command an agricultural hinterland supplying extremely valuable cash crops. Grain, whiskey, and lumber were not the equal of the South's tobacco, cotton, and slaves in building and maintaining a rich, landed aristocracy. Thus the economic base of the founding families rested on comparatively small fortunes, not the incredible wealth that characterized the eastern mercantile elite, the southern planters, or for that matter, the later iron and steel empires on which Pittsburgh's fame rests.

The Arrival and Establishment of the Family Founders

It was into this primitive yet promising milieu that one of the earliest family founders came in 1770, only six years after the Indian siege of Pittsburgh during Pontiac's conspiracy. John Ormsby, college-educated son of a wealthy Scotch-Irish estate holder in Ulster, served as a colonel in the British army during the French and Indian War. In 1770 he was appointed "colonel agent and sole superintendent of the affairs of the Six Nations and other northern Indians."[4] Aided by this official position, Ormsby at once began an extensive and lucrative Indian trade. From the profits gained, he entered other mercantile ventures and by 1776 had become an extensive landholder.

Though he had been born into comfortable circumstances, John Ormsby saw his chance to make his fortune on his own and seized it. And he was not about to lose it; when the ties binding the colonies to Great Britain were imperiled, he adjusted to the changed circumstances. In 1775, he not only dropped his attachments to the crown, but even became a member of a colonial committee of correspondence.

After the Revolutionary War, migration to Southwestern Pennsylvania increased. This was attended by the beginnings of industrialization in the area and the creation of Allegheny County in 1788. A year earlier, John Johnston had arrived in Pittsburgh from Ulster, with his completed apprenticeship to a clockmaker as his only resource. In rented quarters, he began a jewelry, watch, and clock-making business. He prospered and soon erected a three-story building for his business. With demand increasing and materials expensive and difficult to obtain, Johnston began a wire mill with which he supplied himself and other industrial manufacturers. By 1804 he was so well established in the city that he was appointed postmaster of Pittsburgh, a post he held until 1822 when he passed it to his son-in-law as though it were personal property. It is indeed noteworthy that Johnston was able to give the succeeding generation not only his business enterprises, but a federal appointment as well.

By the time John Herron arrived in 1812, Allegheny County had a population of more than twenty-five thousand and was growing at a staggering rate of 6 percent a year. Although the county was predominantly rural, almost one-fifth of its residents lived in Pittsburgh. Before Herron's arrival, other family founders had already changed Pittsburgh: George Anshutz had established an ironworks in 1792; Benjamin Bakewell, a glasshouse in 1808; Alexander Negley, a fulling mill; Rev. Francis Herron, a library company; and Rev. John Wrenshall, the Methodist church.

The second youngest of the family founders, John Herron was twenty years old when he moved to Pittsburgh from Franklin County, Pennsylvania. His position as a clerk in the lumber business marked the beginning of many business ventures. After working for the owner for several years, Herron bought the lumber business and ran it for a time with great success. With his brother-in-law, Col. James Anderson, he purchased the steam saw and gristmill of his father-in-law, Maj. William Anderson. Subsequently, he bought out his brother-in-law as well. To his holdings Herron added a brickyard and used the bricks which it produced and the lumber from his sawmill to begin a contracting and building business. But his ventures were yet far from over. Herron purchased a farm and its coal rights near Pittsburgh, using the coal to supply consumers and his own works. He then bought the sawmill and property of John Irwin and real estate in Pittsburgh. When he acquired half ownership in coal lands on

Turtle Creek, he floated the coal downriver to Pittsburgh, Cincinnati, Louisville, Cairo, and even New Orleans.

Having erected what amounted to a commercial empire, Herron moved to his farm and left the operation of his interests to his sons. His career was the epitome of early founding family diversification.

The three careers of the Ormsby, Johnston, and Herron family founders, while unique, have much in common, and in many ways they typify the larger group of family founders. All three pursued several businesses concurrently and seemed ever on the watch to acquire even more. This process of continually adding another sawmill or another piece of real estate to what they already owned graphically illustrates the concept of the accumulation of advantages. Once a start or main chance was made, the rate at which additional advantages were realized truly suggests an accumulation. It was as though additional wealth-producing properties were acquired geometrically instead of arithmetically, each new holding being more impressive than the previous one.

The original social or economic conditions of the family founders were not, of course, the same. Like Johnston and Herron, most of the founders came to Allegheny County prepared to seize the "break" when it came along. They were ambitious men and they succeeded. Others, such as John Ormsby, used their original position of advantage to gain even more. These three, together with the other family founders, are treated more systematically in figure 2. Along with individual career sketches, a variety of data is given: date and place of birth, date of immigration to America if applicable, date of arrival in Allegheny County, and age at death. It should be noted that two of the families, the Herrons and the Sturgeons, had multiple family founders. The Herrons consisted of two brothers and a cousin; the Sturgeons, three brothers. Although related, they arrived in Allegheny County at separate times. Thus, the twenty founding family surnames actually include twenty-four family founders. In this study each of these extended families is treated as a single lineage.

As the career summaries reveal, the socioeconomic backgrounds of the family founders are as varied as any other aspects of their lives. Still, some observations may be made concerning this inchoate elite, having in common only their early arrival in Allegheny County. In describing the character of the group, it is important to disclaim some popular stereotypes. They are not exclusively the descendants of the English (as opposed to Scottish, Welsh, Scotch-Irish, and Irish) upper class with an aristocratic or merchant-would-be-aristocratic background. Neither do they personify an imagined, stable, eastern class structure, transplanted successfully west of the Appalachians. Nor are they the archetypal western pioneers, breaking out of the class-ridden eastern seaboard and starting fresh, the equal of any other man.

A substantial number of the family founders came with no inherited wealth and achieved their main chance, take-off, or break themselves. These self-made men, along with their well-born counterparts, were able to create a new elite in Allegheny County which was by no means a cohesive or homogeneous class. Indeed, it was as diverse as the population of Allegheny County itself in terms of sophistication, language, heritage, values, religion, and occupation. Even among the nine family founders who were born to wealth there was a considerable amount of cultural diversity. There were also enormous differences in the amount of wealth which their respective families possessed and in the amount of social prestige they could command.

Although the careers of the wealthy were diverse, there was a tendency among them to move into manufacturing, a pursuit requiring a considerable capital outlay. George Anshutz failed at his attempt to process iron near Pittsburgh but started over again in Huntington County in 1795 with a second iron furnace. He had the financial reserves to survive the failure of the previous year when soldiers sent by the new federal government to suppress the Whiskey Rebellion stole his supply of cordwood intended for use as charcoal. Since wood was already becoming scarce in the area east of Pittsburgh where his furnace was located (Shadyside), this

FIGURE 2. Vital Statistics and Career Summaries of the Family Founders

Family Founder	Date of Birth	Age at Death	Place of Birth	If Foreign, Date of Immigration	Date of Arrival in Allegheny Co.	Career Summary
Anshutz, George	1753	84	Alsace, France	1792	1792	Already well off financially when he left Alsace, Anshutz arrived in Pittsburgh to set up an iron furnace. After its failure, he received financial backing to start over in Huntington County where, despite setbacks, he succeeded. He returned to Pittsburgh a wealthy man.
Bakewell, Benjamin	1767	77	Derbyshire, England	1794	1808	Born to a family of cloth importers, Bakewell opened a mercer's business in London at age 23. Upon coming to America he began a brewery in New Haven which was destroyed by fire. A subsequent importing business was ruined by Jefferson's embargo. Finding financial backing from Benjamin Page, he began a successful glasshouse near Pittsburgh. By 1832, Bakewell was sole owner.
Brunot, Felix	1752	86	Morey, France	1777	1797	The foster brother of General Lafayette, Brunot was a surgeon in the army under Washington. After briefly practicing medicine in Annapolis and Philadelphia, he began practice in Pittsburgh, becoming one of its most prominent citizens.

Name	1795/etc	Age	Origin	Description
Denny, Ebenezer	1761	61	Carlisle, Pa.	1795 — Denny came from humble origins. Joining the military, he came to the attention of Gen. St. Clair, was made his aide-de-camp, and was promoted through the ranks to major. After the war he came to Allegheny County to settle on land given him in return for military service. He made additional land purchases and entered politics, becoming treasurer of Allegheny County and the first mayor of Pittsburgh. His old connections brought government favors; he was made commissary of the purchases for troops at Erie and Niagara. He married well.
Dilworth, Samuel	1768	78	Chester Co., Pa.	1795 — On coming to Allegheny County, Dilworth made money by buying a single block of land and selling it in sections. He purchased land along the Ohio River and founded the town of Bellevue, perhaps selling it in lots.
Fahnestock, Samuel	1797	72	Adams Co., Pa.	1818 — Using the knowledge and possibly the financial support of his father who was a merchant and diversified investor, Fahnestock came to Pittsburgh to become an importer and retailer of hardware. He also became involved in insurance and publishing. He married well.

Family Founder	Date of Birth	Age at Death	Place of Birth	If Foreign, Date of Immigration	Date of Arrival in Allegheny Co.	Career Summary
Gilfillan, Alexander,	1746	90	Northern Ireland	ca.1772	1780	After separating from his three brothers who made the passage with him, Gilfillan originally "took" 400 acres of land on Chartiers Creek which he vastly added to in his lifetime. He hired laborers to help him work the land and remained a farmer. Elected the first justice of the peace in St. Clair Township, he held the post for 40 years and was an elder in Mt. Lebanon United Presbyterian Church.
Guthrie, John	1749	103	Lancaster, Pa.		ca.1784	Guthrie rose from humble beginnings to the rank of captain in the military. After the war he came to Allegheny County to take the land given him in return for military service. He also became a builder and for a time manufactured rope.
Herron, Rev. Francis	1774	86	Shippensburg, Pa.		1811	Francis Herron took his D.D. degree from Dickinson College. Apparently he had some money of his own, since on coming to Pittsburgh, he bought the First Presbyterian Church when it was sold for taxes and donated it back to the congregation. He was pastor for 49 years, helped establish Western Theological Seminary, and was elected to state office.

Name					
Herron, John	1792	71	Franklin Co., Pa.	1812	John Herron began as a clerk in the lumber business. He parlayed his money and bought the lumber business. With his brother-in-law he bought his father-in-law's steam saw- and grist-mills, then bought out his brother-in-law. Later he added a brickyard and did building and contracting. After acquiring coal rights in Minersville, he supplied coal to consumers and his own works. He began buying property and a sawmill in Pittsburgh. With his son and W. A. Brown, he began a huge coal mining and supply business which extended to New Orleans. He married well.
Herron, William	ca.1793	—	Cumberland Co., Pa.	ca.1814	The brother of John and cousin of Francis, William Herron became a farmer and landowner in Allegheny County. He prospered and moved to Chippewa Township in Beaver County where he continued farming.
Johnston, John	1765	62	Co. Antrim, No. Ireland	1787	From humble beginnings as a clockmaker's apprentice, Johnston came to Pittsburgh and rented quarters to set up a jewelry, watch, and clockmaking business. He soon erected a three-story building for his business. To supply his needs and those of other manufacturers, he started a wire mill. Among government favors received was an appointment as postmaster of Pittsburgh from 1804 to 1822 with which his daughter "assisted." He married well.

Family Founder	Date of Birth	Age at Death	Place of Birth	If Foreign, Date of Immigration	Date of Arrival in Allegheny Co.	Career Summary
Liggett, Robert	1743	63	Co. Antrim, No. Ireland	1771	1781	From humble beginnings Liggett became a farmer and landowner in Chester County, later acquiring a farm in Finleyville. His wife was from the prominent Darragh family and was the sister of Pittsburgh's second mayor.
McClure, John	1723	88	Carlisle, Pa.		1760	Having inherited much land and a manor house from his father, who had purchased 6,475 acres from the Penns, McClure became a successful Pittsburgh merchant. He received government favors, including the contract to supply Fort Pitt, which he used to advantage. He managed abandoned Fort McIntosh for the government. He invested successfully in large tracts of land, becoming a country gentleman. He married well.
Negley, Alexander	1734	75	near Frankfort, Germany	1739	1778	From humble beginnings as a blacksmith and private in the Revolution, Negley came to East Liberty at an early date (the first white settler) and took 300 acres. He erected a gristmill and fulling mills and added to his landholdings.
Neville, John	1731	72	Occoquan, Va.		1783	Born of a prominent Virginia family, Neville became a general during the Revolution. After the war he came to Pittsburgh as inspector of revenue. He paid for the erection of the first Episco-

Name	Birth	Age	Origin			
						pal church west of the mountains. He and his wife, daughter of a prominent Virginia family, lived at his Bower Hill estate and Pittsburgh townhouse. After the war he had no real occupation, but was wealthy and prestigious.
Nimick, William	ca. 1785	ca. 67	Northern Ireland	1815	1819	From humble beginnings Nimick accumulated enough money to become a grocer, then a wholesale grocer and merchant. He was considered a "gentleman" by his neighbors.
Ormsby, John	1720	85	Northern Ireland	1752	1770	A college graduate, Ormsby was born on the family estate held since James I. Coming to America as agent in charge of Indian affairs, he began an extensive and lucrative Indian trade, obviously aided by his official position. He also held vast lands south of Pittsburgh and entered other mercantile ventures. He married well.
Page, Benjamin	1765	69	Norwich, England	1797	1814	At age 20 Page inherited a considerable amount of property. Upon coming to America he became an importer until the embargo, during and after which he invested in Bakewell's glasshouse.
Phillips, John	1750	84	Northern Ireland	before 1776	ca.1802	Coming from a military family, Phillips began as a private but rose to rank of major in the New Jersey militia. After the Revolution, he became the sheriff of Hunterdon County, N.J. He married the colonel's daughter. He is a descendant of a Puritan clergyman who emigrated to America in 1630; his father's circumstances are unknown.

Family Founder	Date of Birth	Age at Death	Place of Birth	If Foreign, Date of Immigration	Date of Arrival in Allegheny Co.	Career Summary
Sturgeon, Henry	1754	94	York Co., Pa.		1790	Henry Sturgeon followed his brothers to the area where he became a farmer owning 400 acres in Oakdale. He served as first lieutenant in the York County militia during the Revolution.
Sturgeon, Jeremiah	1760	56	York Co., Pa.		1780	The first of three brothers from a middle-class family to arrive in Pittsburgh, Jeremiah Sturgeon was a blacksmith in York County. He purchased a hotel in Pittsburgh where he prospered and became very wealthy.
Sturgeon, William	1756	80	York Co., Pa.		ca. 1785	Following his brother's lead, William bought a farm in Oakdale where he prospered.
Wrenshall, John	1761	60	Preston, England	1794	1796	Son of a family in the mercantile business, Wrenshall had an educated, upper-middle-class background. After being spurned by his family for leaving the Anglican church, he went to Philadelphia preaching Methodism and became a wealthy merchant. He came to Pittsburgh to preach and to become a merchant, though he had already made his money. He married well.

presented a major blow to his enterprise. Yet he persisted in manufacturing because he had access to the credit and financial backing that was available to the wealthy. He eventually succeeded and was able to ship iron to Pittsburgh. Although Anshutz lived in Huntington County for thirty-eight years, his children lived in Pittsburgh, and he returned permanently in 1833.[5]

The ability to draw on personal connections and the capital they provided distinguishes family founders of wealthy parentage from those who were born to humble circumstances. The two wealthy family founders who pursued mercantile interests, John Ormsby and John McClure, were able to use their wealth and connections to secure large contracts. This contrasts sharply with their middle-class counterparts, John Herron and William Nimick, who started as shopkeeper and grocer respectively. Though they all ended up wealthy, some had to work harder to get there.

It was only among the wealthy family founders that non-business professional careers (physician, minister, and government official) were pursued. Well-secured by their own private resources, Dr. Felix Brunot, Rev. Francis Herron, and Gen. John Neville were ensconced comfortably in the highest social positions which their respective professions afforded. Brunot was the most distinguished physician in Pittsburgh, Herron possibly the most esteemed minister, and Neville was as close to being an aristocrat as republican America west of the Alleghenies would allow.[6]

The relationship of the family founders to government at all levels is an interesting one and worked to their advantage in two ways. They were able to obtain the positions they desired in the government, and then to use them to advance their own fortunes. John McClure is an excellent example of this. The son of a landowner who was well connected with the Penns, he was elected coroner of Cumberland County, Pennsylvania, in 1753. Although he served only two terms, it was long enough to give him intimacy in his own right with men of power and influence. Gambling on the prospect of still greater opportunities west of the Alleghenies, at age thirty-seven he obtained a contract from the British government to furnish supplies to Fort Pitt. The earliest of any family founder to arrive in the area, McClure came to Fort Pitt in 1760 with five of his six children and his wife Martha, who was the sister of another family founder, Ebenezer Denny. McClure formed a mutually beneficial relationship with a third family founder, John Ormsby. Ormsby's virtual monopoly over the Indian trade coincided nicely with McClure's control of the supplies coming into Fort Pitt. Ormsby supplied McClure, and together the two made a lot of money in a hurry.[7]

What they did with the money was what many rich colonial merchants did: they invested it in land. John McClure acquired tracts of land in three different locations and as far away as the upper Susquehanna watershed. John Ormsby was also a large landholder by 1776, owning potentially valuable tracts across the Monongahela River from Pittsburgh. Its value increased when he began a ferry service.[8]

When the American Revolution swept away the imperial government, neither man seemed to have had much trouble switching alliances. They had no intention of backing the losing side; none of the family founders did. When the Revolutionary War ended in 1783 the government abandoned Fort McIntosh on the Ohio at the mouth of the Beaver River. John McClure was able to use his connections to be appointed manager of that inactive fort. The position was practically a sinecure, but it afforded additional income that enabled him to increase his landholdings just three years later. In 1786 he purchased a tract of land near Homestead on the Monongahela River. Calling it Amity Plantation, John McClure lived out the rest of his life—he was to live for another twenty-five years—in the style of a country gentleman, complete with hounds.

The family founders were unanimously committed to the revolutionary cause. John Neville, who had served with Washington in the Braddock expedition, was made a general in the Continental Army. Dr. Felix Brunot came to America with his foster brother Lafayette to serve as a surgeon under Washington. In order of rank, Maj. John Phillips, Capt. John Guthrie, 1st Lt. Henry Sturgeon, Pvt. Alexander Negley, and Jeremiah Sturgeon (rank unknown) all served in the Revolutionary War. Many of these may have received land as partial payment for their service.

If the family founders demonstrated wisdom in backing the winning side in the Revolution, they were to prove equally wise during the Whiskey Rebellion of 1794. Reaction against Hamilton's federal tax on distilled spirits was particularly strong in Western Pennsylvania because the area was economically dependent on the export of rye whiskey. Gen. John Neville, collector of the whiskey revenue in Southwestern Pennsylvania, became a focus of the farmers' anger. They burned his mansion, Bower Hill, before marching on Pittsburgh in a show of force.[9] Family founder Alexander Gilfillan, although a justice of the peace, was not in the service of the federal government. Yet he refused to join his enraged neighbors. The rebels marked his barn to be burned, but they never returned. Likewise, John Ormsby sided with the federal government, but he managed to stay on the sidelines. William McClure (1750–1815), son of family founder John McClure, did side with the rebels, but only to the point of not endorsing the measure taken by the federal government to suppress them. Most of the founding families wisely kept a very low profile throughout the crisis.

The family founders who came from truly humble origins— the self-made men—frequently chose the military as an initial path to upward mobility. Those with some cash reserves were more likely to go into farming or business. Farming evolved into landholding, a business developed into multifaceted enterprises, and sometimes the two were linked in a symbiotic relationship. Alexander Negley's career embraced the military, business, and farming. This German-born blacksmith, who may have initially obtained property in the form of a land grant given to Revolutionary War veterans, moved into the business sector by erecting a gristmill and a fulling mill while continuing to add to his landholdings.[10]

Ebenezer Denny's involvement in the military led his career in a different direction. Coming from extremely humble conditions, he obtained employment as a bearer of dispatches to Fort Pitt at the age of thirteen. During the Revolutionary War, he volunteered to serve on a privateer bound for the West Indies and became an ensign. He attracted the attention of Gen. Arthur St. Clair who made him an aide-de-camp. He progressed up the ranks to major. In 1795 he left the military to come to Allegheny County where he became prominent in government service. He served as county commissioner and in 1803 and 1808 was elected county treasurer. His military and political connections enabled him to become commissary of purchases for troops at Erie and Niagara during the War of 1812. After a spectacular climb from the poverty of his boyhood, he was elected the first mayor of Pittsburgh in 1816. Denny's career exemplifies how important the role of the military—and government—could be in providing the ladder by which self-made men could climb to relative greatness.[11]

Most of the family founders who settled in rural Allegheny County belong to the self-made group, since the wealthy seemed to consider land speculation only as a secondary interests once their fortunes had been established. The middle-class family founders tended to use land as an opportunity for investment to a far greater degree. Alexander Gilfillan, William Herron, Henry Sturgeon, and William Sturgeon all continued to farm the land as their primary occupation.[12]

The economic origins of the family founders were closely related to their ethnic origins. More than half of them were foreign-born, but immigrant or nonimmigrant, their economic status was related to nationality. Nearly half were Scotch-Irish, a proportion not markedly different from the population of Allegheny County as a whole at the time; the presence of so many Scotch-Irish in this sample should not be considered unrepresentative of the elite in the county. Indeed, the county itself was atypical of the larger American society.[13] The large number of Scotch-Irish in the area constituted not merely an ethnic difference, but an economic difference as well. Since Ulster did not produce great landed or mercantile wealth, those emigrating from that unhappy region brought little financial reserve. Of the nine Scotch-Irish founding families, only John Ormsby and Rev. Francis Herron possessed any significant wealth. The rest were self-made men, initially lacking the capital essential for successful entrepreneurship. Although not even the Scotch-Irish could be described as lower class, it is among this group that nearly all the men of humble beginnings can be found.

Typical of this group is Robert Liggett, who immigrated from County Antrim in 1771 at the age of twenty-eight. After three years' labor he was able to acquire a 150-acre farm in Chester County, Pennsylvania. Liggett moved to Pittsburgh in 1778, one of the earlier family founders in the area. The following year he had the good fortune to marry Isabella Darragh whose brother was to become the second mayor of Pittsburgh. Profiting from his connections with the Darragh family, he acquired land south of the city. Like so many other family founders, his success was based on the gradual accumulation of property combined with a propitious marriage.[14]

In contrast to the Scotch-Irish, the English came to Allegheny County with wealth and connections already established. Family traditions of investment in mercantile ventures, profiting from Great Britain's rise to commercial dominance, led to personal fortunes which were often considerable. These family founders, though born with the accumulation of advantages well established, were not the stereotypical ne'er-do-well scions of successful forebears, content to live off rents or allowances. Rather, their careers were marked by industry and vision.

Benjamin Page, born Benjamin Jagger in Norwich, England, in 1765, assumed his mother's maiden name at age twenty as a condition for claiming a large inheritance from her family. Having realized the main chance in this unorthodox manner, Page opened a London counting house the following year. Seeking to increase his wealth and put his expertise and connections to good use, he moved his family to New York in 1797 where he became an importer of English goods. By 1807, however, Page's importing business had been adversely affected by Jefferson's embargo. His estate remained intact, however, and when Benjamin Bakewell (another family founder), also an importer and a close friend, proposed the profitability of a glass manufacturing establishment in Pittsburgh, Page agreed to back him. Jefferson's embargo was followed by yet another restraint on trade, the War of 1812. Page, who had continued to live in New York, decided to follow his investment to Pittsburgh in 1814. The Bakewell glasshouse prospered, increasing Page's wealth until 1832 when he sold out entirely to Bakewell. Benjamin Page was now sixty-seven; his health was not good. He also had established himself as one of the city's socially prominent citizens—the manager of the Pittsburgh Permanent Library Association and a manager of the Pittsburgh Bible Society. Despite these and other connections (most of his twelve children were grown and one had even married a Bakewell), Benjamin Page moved to Cincinnati. He died two years later. Page's career is unique in that he left Allegheny County. Yet his pursuit of opportunity is symbolic of all the family founders. What counted was not place or emotional attachments, but new chances to be pursued with energy and ambition. Page left Pittsburgh for the same reasons he left Norwich, London, and New York. Even with fortune already in hand, he could not ignore the lure of new business opportunities whenever they presented themselves.[15]

Although the majority of the founding families were either Scotch-Irish or English, five were German, Scottish, or French (all of them, except one, from wealthy circumstances). For the Germans and the French, the existence of a different language, religion, and cultural tradition created additional barriers to success. This point should not be overemphasized, however, especially with regard to the Germans, who constituted about a third of the population in Pennsylvania. But there was an unwritten distinction between being tolerated as part of the economic elite and being socially assimilated into the prevailing English-speaking Protestant culture. Dr. Felix Brunot, despite his close relationship to Lafayette, his medical service under Washington, and his professional status as a physician, still felt it necessary to leave the Roman Catholic church for the Anglican in order to win social acceptance.

Nor did Samuel Fahnestock, son of a Pennsylvania Dutch merchant and turnpike owner, cleave to a German-speaking church congregation. Fahnestock, born in Adams County, Pennsylvania, in 1797, was the last born of the family founders. He came to Pittsburgh in 1818 with his wife, Eliza Heyser, to become an importer of hardware and cutlery. When his first wife, who was of German descent, died in 1836, he married Mary Murray. Her father, Magnus Murray, a noted lawyer, and her mother, Mary Wilkins, were both from prominent families (listed in Powelson's index). This second marriage could be interpreted as a shedding of his foreignness as well as an indication of his own acceptance by the dominant culture. It is significant that after this second marriage, Fahnestock entered the insurance business. In 1850 he published a city directory for Pittsburgh. Secure in his social position he even had his portrait painted by the celebrated artist Rembrandt Peale. For Samuel Fahnestock, business success opened the doors to social acceptance and social conformity led to still greater business success.[16]

Religion played an interesting role in bringing some of the family founders to the area. Several of them were freethinkers whose ideas on religion conflicted with the established churches of their forefathers. Socially ostracized or discredited by their participation in small sects, many of them left their native communities. Even the successful merchant-minister, Rev. John Wrenshall, left England because his family disapproved of his leaving the Anglican church for the Methodist. He came to Pittsburgh to preach Methodism, supporting himself by mercantile investments since his Methodist parishioners were generally not among the wealthy.[17] Benjamin Page, a Presbyterian, was excluded from communion in England and left the church. His first wife, whom he married in New York, was a Methodist. John Herron was a trustee of his Presbyterian church in Northern Ireland, but it was a Seceder sect. Although most of the family founders belonged to the more socially acceptable Anglican and Presbyterian churches, the number of family founders who had radically divergent views shows a strong individualism in this generation.

Table 1 gives the ethnic origins of the family founders and lists them according to the economic status to which they were born.

More than half the family founders were foreign-born, and they arrived in America over a long period of time. Alexander Negley came in 1739 as a child of five. William Nimick, the last to arrive, came from Northern Ireland in 1815 at the age of thirty. John Herron came directly to Allegheny County from County Down, Northern Ireland, in 1810, but most of the other immigrants stayed elsewhere and moved to the Pittsburgh area four years to twenty years later.

Migration to Allegheny County covered a period of sixty

TABLE 1
Ethnic and Social Origins of the Family Founders

	Wealthy	Middle-class	"Humble"	Unknown
Scotch-Irish	Ormsby Herron[a]	Gilfillan Herron[a] Sturgeon	Denny Guthrie Johnston Liggett Nimick	
English	Bakewell Neville Page Wrenshall			Dilworth[b] Phillips[c]
German	Anshutz Fahnestock		Negley	
Scottish	McClure			
French	Brunot			

a. Two of the three Herrons were middle class; one was wealthy.

b. Samuel Dilworth was born of Quaker parents in a town named for the family. At twenty-eight years of age he purchased nearly a thousand acres of land near Pittsburgh. Thus it is unlikely that he came from "humble" circumstances.

c. John Phillips was probably not from "humble" circumstances.

years. The dates of arrival are largely clustered in two separated time periods: 1778–1797 and 1809–1819. By all indications, virtually no economic advantage accrued to the earlier arrivals, contrary to popular belief. It is commonly held that, in the American experience, the first settlers in a given community acquired all or nearly all the desirable land and profited from its increased values as the population grew. Although in the case of the founding families the earlier arrivals were indeed large landowners, Allegheny County was destined to become an urban center based on commerce and manufacturing rather than on agriculture. The agricultural hinterland was important in supplying the needs of Pittsburgh, but even this did not yield profits comparable to those realized by southern planters. The immense increase in population in the nineteenth century would render these lands, and especially those holdings close to burgeoning Pittsburgh, quite valuable. By then, however, the profits from sales would be divided among the numerous descendants of the family founders. Apparently Samuel Dilworth was the only family founder to have profited greatly from his land sales. He sold his extensive holdings south of the city in four separate sales to the Boggs family between 1796 and 1799.[18]

The family founders who arrived between 1809 and 1819 were more involved in commerce and manufacturing. If landholding afforded the earlier arrivals no immediate fortunes, neither did these enterprises yield enormous profits to the later arrivals. These merchants and manufacturers operated on a small scale compared to their eastern contemporaries. The relatively small population and limited markets restricted the possibility of amassing the truly large fortunes that were then being made in New York, Philadelphia, Boston, and Baltimore. Thus the obligation of making the accumulation of advantages work was as pressing for their children as it was for the family founders themselves.

Perhaps one of the most striking facts concerning the family founders, and contributing greatly to their success and that of their children, was their longevity. Every one of the family founders lived longer than the normal life expectancy.

As a group, they lived 77.6 years, far in excess of the average life expectancy at that time (see appendix). Their lives were characterized by long working careers and, in some cases, no retirement at all. This in itself would have allowed more than sufficient time for capital accumulation. It would have aided those families with business interests by providing continuity of management and the advantages which long associations with customers and other businesses often bring. The benefits received by the second generation due to the longevity of the first were of enormous significance and value.

George Anshutz, Jr., son of the family founder, acted for most of his life as his father's agent in Pittsburgh, retailing the ironware which his father produced in Huntington County. George, Jr., was fifty-six when his father died. Oliver Ormsby, son of John, continued his father's trading business in northwestern Pennsylvania and used it as a springboard to establish still more stores at Erie and Niagara. Oliver's business association with his father lasted until his father's death when Oliver was thirty-eight. His long apprenticeship having served him well, Oliver branched out into still more successful business ventures. The benefits bestowed by longevity were shared by the professionals as well. Dr. Felix Brunot's son James learned medicine from his father before leaving Pittsburgh for the South in order to begin his own practice. These instances are typical of some of the advantages conferred on the second generation by the extreme longevity of the first.

As has been shown, the family founders were a diverse group of economically and socially prominent individuals. They differed in ethnicity, religion, economic origins, occupational pursuits, and dates of arrival to Allegheny County. But their characters were similarly marked by driving ambition and the ability to seize opportunities when they occurred. All were looking for the main chance, even those who supposedly did not require it. Diverse as they were, they formed an identifiable, if inchoate, economic elite. In 1820 this elite was by no means the social upper class that would later be created. Nonetheless, even in this formative period, there were undefined, subtle pressures in the direction of cultural conformity, particularly in regard to religion. Some family founders experienced these pressures and chose to resist them, but most did not. For the time being, at least, social considerations were not paramount. What mattered most was achieving economic success by whatever avenue available. For the founding families, this avenue took them to Allegheny County. In this search for something better, they were not too much unlike the rest of those who came; they reflected the cultural diversity of the larger population which was struggling to establish a social, economic, and political order where none had existed half a century before. It is therefore necessary to describe the general population and to place the founding families in this setting in 1820 at the close of the arrival period.

IV

The Founding Families in 1820

Population

I N   1 8 2 0 , Allegheny County was still far from the importance it was destined to attain in the state and the nation. While
the U.S. population for that year was reported at 9,638,453,
with 1,049,458 in Pennsylvania, the population of Allegheny
County was only 34,921, just 0.3 percent of the nation. However, both the county and Pittsburgh were growing at a rate far
outstripping that of the United States and Pennsylvania. In
1820 the population of Pittsburgh was 7,248, a 52 percent increase from the previous decade.[1] But this high growth rate
was not extraordinary for western cities at this time. In fact the
six-year depression following the Panic of 1819 seriously re-
tarded Pittsburgh's economic development and its population
growth as well. As a consequence, Pittsburgh yielded its first-
place position among western cities to its downriver rival, Cincinnati. Compounding the ill effects of the depression, the
construction of the National Road and the Erie Canal both
tended to divert traffic from the area. Nonetheless, Pittsburgh
experienced a population increase of 73 percent in the 1820s,
raising it to 12,450 inhabitants by 1830.[2] In that year the *Pittsburgh Gazette* estimated the population of Pittsburgh and its
environs at 25,000, including the towns of Allegheny, Birming-
ham, Bayardstown, Lawrenceville, and East Liberty.[3]

In the twenty years from 1810 to 1830 the census revealed an enormous rate of city growth; Pittsburgh tripled in size while Pennsylvania did not quite double its population. Allegheny County, exclusive of Pittsburgh, also experienced a burgeoning population, though it too lagged behind the city. Table 2 illustrates the absolute and relative rates of growth in the city and county.

Children and young adults constituted the bulk of the American population in 1820. In Allegheny County nearly half the population was under sixteen years of age, though for Pittsburgh this percentage was slightly lower. By contrast, only 12 percent of the county's population was forty-five or older. The founding families had a slightly older age structure. They were most at variance with the larger population in the percentage of children under sixteen. While over 47 percent of the county was under sixteen, only 40 percent of the founding family members fell within that age group. Table 3 gives the distribution of the population by age for Allegheny County and the founding families in 1820. It reveals that while founding family birth rates were somewhat lower than the larger population, generally they resembled the county population.

Among the 230 founding family members living in 1820 whose place of birth is known, 29 (12.6 percent) were foreign-born. Of these, 37.9 percent were over forty-five; only 10.3 percent were under seventeen.[4] By 1820, the immigrant founding family members were an aging minority. Time had consid-

TABLE 2
Population Growth in Pittsburgh and Allegheny County, 1810–1830

	County Population	% Increase	City Population	% Increase	City Population as % of County
1810	25,317	68	4,768	205	19
1820	34,921	38	7,248	52	21
1830	50,552	45	12,450	73	25

TABLE 3
Age Distribution, 1820

	Age Groups				
	0–15	16–25	26–44	45+	Total
Allegheny County	47% (16,100)	22% (7,400)	19% (6,500)	12% (4,100)	100% (34,100)
Founding families	40% (46)	22% (25)	23% (27)	15% (17)	100% (115)

Note: Year of birth is known for almost all the core group, but is unknown for many non-core husbands.

erably localized the founding families as nearly half of them in this time period had been born in Allegheny County.

Economic Base

By 1820 Pittsburgh had already become a significant manufacturing center. Three hundred fifty-four men, 141 children and 2 women produced $2,553,549 worth of goods annually.[5] Protected by the mountains from eastern and foreign competition, a vigorous iron industry developed, made possible by local coal and iron deposits. Iron and iron products accounted for 46 percent of the value of the city's manufactures and employed 28.8 percent of the manufacturing population. So preeminent was the iron industry as early as 1820 that the next five in rank order of importance—leather, cotton goods, lumber processing, glass, and paper—constituted less than one-third of the value of manufactured goods. Despite the importance of manufacturing, it could not have employed more than 6 percent of the county's adult male population or 20 percent of the city's. Table 4 is a listing of industries in the county according to annual output. It also gives the number of persons employed in manufacturing alone.

Commerce was probably of even greater importance than manufacturing in terms of persons employed. *The Pittsburgh*

TABLE 4
Manufacturing Industries in Allegheny County, 1820

Industry	Value of Annual Production	% of Total Value of Annual Production	Number Employed	% of Total Number Employed
Iron	$ 559,000	21.89	83	17
Nails	309,000	12.10	36	7
Leather goods	236,000	9.24	43	9
Cotton goods	200,000	7.83	14	3
Lumber	177,000	6.93	9	2
Steam engines	152,800	5.99	12	2
Castings	132,610	5.20	10	2
Glass	131,804	5.16	64	13
Paper	82,400	3.23	38	8
Smithwork	82,000	3.21	27	5
Liquors (all)	60,000	2.35	44	9
Tobacco products	53,000	2.08	52	10
Flour	36,000	1.41	16	3
Woolen goods	33,667	1.32	23	5
Rope, twine	15,000	0.59	12	2
Wire work	10,000	0.39	2	1
Miscellaneous	282,780	11.08	12	2
Total	$2,553,549	100.00	497	100

Sources: U.S. Census Office, *Fourth Census,* 1820; and Sarah H. Killikelly, *The History of Pittsburgh: Its Rise and Progress* (Pittsburgh: B. C. Gordon Montgomery Co., 1906), p. 166.

Directory for 1815 listed 122 merchants and 82 store and hotel owners.[6] The merchants served far more than the local market, for Pittsburgh had already become a gateway to the West. As early as 1785 the *Pittsburgh Gazette* (February 7) estimated that 13,000 people had passed through the town in 1784, a number that increased dramatically in succeeding years. Almost all these pioneers required provisions from local merchants, many of whom were founding family members. In addition to the products of local factories and farms, the merchants also handled goods from the East and from abroad, since Pittsburgh was a transfer point from land to water transportation for downriver communities.[7] The rivers aided Pittsburgh's growth perhaps even more than its surrounding coal deposits. The Ohio and Mississippi rivers provided inexpensive highways of commerce to the interior and to the South. By 1820 a considerable volume of downriver and an increasing amount of upriver traffic had developed as a result of the introduction of the steamboat.[8] Pittsburgh's fledgling manufacturing and commercial interests thus developed in the still largely rural county.

While no agricultural census exists for this period, the raw materials produced in the hinterlands and finished in Pittsburgh are recorded in the manufacturing census. Allegheny County's flour industry consumed more than 100,000 bushels of wheat annually, making that the region's most widely grown cash crop. Nine tanneries used 6,720 hides per year, the county's third most important industry. This was followed by lumber (3 sawmills), liquor, and tobacco. Despite the fact that about 70 percent of the county's population was rural and chiefly engaged in agriculture, the combined market of the five industries listed above yielded less income than the iron industry alone.[9]

The founding family members, which by this time included male descendants (core) and daughters' husbands and children (non-core), were widely distributed among the various occupations but not in proportion to the total population. They were concentrated almost exclusively in occupations which yielded a good income and prestige. It is in this most critical aspect that the founding families manifested their high socioeconomic position within the class structure. Their dominance in the professional, commercial, and manufacturing fields was complemented by similar positions in the government and military. Those who were farmers held land far in excess of what any single individual in preindustrial times could possibly cultivate. The farm typically embraced well over three hundred and fifty acres. In addition, every founding family farmer for whom information is available held interests outside agriculture, such as a local government post (Alexander Gilfillan and William McClure were both justices of the peace) or in a related industry (Alexander Negley operated a gristmill and fulling mill). Still others were able to secure government contracts (John McClure furnished supplies for the garrison at Fort Pitt and later managed abandoned Fort McIntosh for the government). But for most, simply holding their large tracts represented an investment as land values increased. Clearly, all the family founders engaged in agriculture in 1820 were in the upper echelons of the rural social structure.

The majority of the founding family members, however, engaged in urban-oriented occupations and lived in or near the city of Pittsburgh in 1820. Of the 227 who were adults in 1820 (age seventeen and over), more than 12 percent were professionals. Of these, about one-half were doctors or lawyers. The rest were clergymen, authors, teachers, an engineer, and a scientist. The typical urbanite was engaged in a commercial activity. Forty-six, or about 20 percent, fell into this category, which included merchants, commission merchants, bankers, shipper/wholesalers, and real estate agents. The production of goods engaged another 17 percent, most often processing a food or product. This usually involved the operation of a flour or lumber mill. Of the thirty-five who at one time or another were in the military, all but two were officers. Considering the size of the military as a percentage of the total U.S. population even during the Revolution, the percentage among founding families, 15, is quite large. The families are underrepresented in the clerical and mechanical occupations, only eight. Since the term *clerk* at this time gave little indication of income or responsibility, the two who remained clerks may or may not have achieved a higher position within the designation.[10] The other six were young and later moved on to what could clearly be recognized as more rewarding occupations. The same applied to those individuals holding lower ranking positions in the military.

Table 5 illustrates more carefully the distribution of the founding families among various occupations. Ninety-nine persons representing 227 occupations are listed. This is so because some engaged in two distinct occupations at once,

TABLE 5
Occupation Distribution of Founding Family Members Age 17 and Over,
Compared to the *Pittsburgh City Directory*, 1815

Occupation	Founding Family		Pittsburgh City Directory	
	No.	%	No.	%
Professional	28	12.3	48	3
Judge			1	
Lawyer	7		12	
Doctor	6		8	
Clergy	5		8	
Editor/author	5		2	
Teacher/professor	3		8	
Engineer	1		9	
Scientist	1			
Commercial	46	20.2	238	19
Banker	5		5	
Merchant	9			
Commission Merchant	6		125	
Shipper/wholesaler	7			
Real estate dealer	5		3	
Agent	3			
Store owner	9			
Druggist	1		105	
Hotel owner	1			
Production (entreprenurial)	39	17.1	35	3
Manufacturer (unspecified)	9			
Iron manfucturer	5		19	
Glass manufacturer	3			
Food/product processor[a]	11		10[b]	
Printer	1		5	
Builder/contractor	7		1	
Mine owner/operator	3			
Clerical/Mechanical	8	3.5	675	55
Bookkeeper	1		8	
Clerk	4		29	
Mechanic	3		331[c]	
Laborer	0		289[d]	
Foreman	0		18	

Occupation	Founding Family		Pittsburgh City Directory	
	No.	%	No.	%
Farming/Landholding	47	20.6	2	—
Farmer	27			
Landowner	20			
Government	23	10.1	23	2
Senator	1		1	
State official	9			
Local official	13		22e	
Military	35	15.3	19f	2
General	1			
Colonel	6			
Major	10			
Captain	7			
1st Lieut.	4			
2nd Lieut.	5			
Private	2			
Other	2	0.9		
Female (not employed)	1	0.5	102	8
Gentleman	—		36	3
No occupation listed	—		58	5
Total	228	100.0	1236	100.0

a. Flour and saw mills.
b. Includes brewing, distilling, and bottling.
c. Skilled worker.
d. Unskilled worker.
e. Includes 6 justices of the peace.
f. Military rank was not always specified.

both of which contributed significantly to his income. Oliver Ormsby was at once a commission merchant, a director of the Pittsburgh branch of the U.S. Bank, and owner of a flour mill in Cincinnati, a cotton factory and rope walk in Chillicothe, Ohio, a grist and sand mill, and a forge and iron furnace in Beaver Falls, Pennsylvania. He simultaneously continued his father's trading business at Erie and Niagara. While he is unusual, he illustrates the varied interests in which the founding families were likely to be engaged. Therefore table 5 does not confine itself to only one of an individual's occupations. As in Ormsby's case, it is sometimes impossible to determine a primary occupation.

While showing the distribution of the founding family members among the occupations, table 5 also compares this distribution with that of the 1815 *Pittsburgh Directory*. This privately published directory alphabetically listed all adult men and unmarried women along with their occupations and addresses. Since it was intended to be comprehensive, it was in no way an elite listing. Laborers were included equally with lawyers. The directory also listed individuals in various stages of their life cycles. Those listed as laborers in 1815 were not necessarily confined to that occupation for the rest of their lives. Because the city directory was of an almost entirely urban group (12 percent of the founding family members in this period were farmers), numerous characteristics distinguish those listed in the directory from the founding families.

Of the seven major occupational groups, only the commercial classification engaged similar proportions of both the founding families and the people listed in the directory. At this time Pittsburgh was still an essentially commercial city. The percentage designated as commercial was inflated due to the inclusion in the directory of literally everyone engaged in commerce, such as tavernkeepers and owners of livery stables. The percent of founding family members in commerce was actually higher vis-à-vis the city directory group, since they were usually not engaged in such occupations so tenuously related to commerce.

More than four times as many founding family members were concentrated in the professions as were listed in the city directory. More than 3 percent were lawyers, for instance, as compared to less than 1 percent in the directory. The difference between the respective groups of manufacturers was even greater. Small as their group was, more founding family members were manufacturers or engaged in related occupations than the number of manufacturers listed in the entire city directory. The same was true of the military. In government their numbers were equal.

Among the lower-status occupations, clerical/mechanical, the situation was completely reversed. Of the eight founding family members in this classification (about 4 percent of the total), most were clerks and bookkeepers. None were laborers, although this designation embraced 55 percent of those listed in the city directory. Clearly, the founding families in 1820 had firmly established themselves among the city's occupational elite even as they had among the county's rural elite.

Government

Allegheny County was created in 1788 from parts of Westmoreland and Washington counties. It extended as far north as the New York state border until 1803 when it was reduced to its present 730.4 square miles. Under the provisions of the Pennsylvania constitution of 1776, the administration of a county rested with a board of county commissioners elected directly by the people for a three-year term. Assessors, a recorder of deeds, and register of wills were also directly elected; the sheriff and coroner were to be commissioned annually by the president in council from two elected nominees. Six road viewers responsible for road construction and vacating of property continued to be appointed by the county court as they had been in the past.

In 1789 a criminal court was established. The state constitution of 1790 made each county a part of a judicial circuit headed by a president judge. The county itself was permitted to have no fewer than three nor more than four judges. Three auditors were appointed by these judges to "audit, settle and adjust the public accounts of the treasurer and commissioners." Prothonotaries, "clerks of the peace and orphans' courts," were appointed by the governor.

The constitution of 1790 abolished township overseers of the poor and placed responsibility in the hands of elected county poor directors. In the first of a long series of democratizing tendencies it also provided for the direct election of auditors.[11]

Pittsburgh, a village since its founding in 1758, was incorporated as a borough in 1794. In 1816 the citizens asked for and received a city charter. It allowed a government consisting of a mayor, a Select Council and a Common Council, all of which were elective. In addition to his executive authority, the mayor was empowered to try cases involving forgery, perjury, larceny, assault, and battery. A recorder, twelve aldermen, and a clerk of the mayor's court were appointed by the governor.[12]

Seven townships were formed in Allegheny County in 1788: Monongahela, St. Clair, Mifflin, Elizabeth, Versailles, Plum, and Pitt. Many of these were subdivided in the late eighteenth and early nineteenth centuries, especially in areas adjacent to Pittsburgh. While some were distinctly urban, sharing in Pittsburgh's social and economic life, the city of Pittsburgh did not annex any land until 1837 when the state passed an enabling act permitting the residents of the Northern Liberties to vote upon annexation. This annexation created no rush to join the city and annexations continued at a slow pace.[13]

Unlike the Philadelphia upper class, Allegheny County's founding families were not chary of public office. In Pittsburgh the lists of officials occupying the offices of mayor, city council, and school board are replete with founding family names.[14] Among the rural families, the elected office of justice of the peace was a favorite. The county judicial position of judge of the Court of Common Pleas was especially coveted, and judges became important local and even statewide figures.[15] A partial selection of core member officeholders at this time included family founder Ebenezer Denny, who was elected the first mayor of Pittsburgh in 1816; Morgan Neville (1783–1840), who held the post of sheriff of Allegheny County from 1819 to 1822; Felix Brunot, Jr. (1794–1827), who served as deputy attorney general for Allegheny County; James V. Guthrie (1778–1827), who was a city constable;[16] and William Sturgeon (1792–1883), who served two terms in the state legislature. Daniel

Sturgeon (1789–1878) began a long political career during this period that started with his election to the state legislature in 1819. After serving three terms, he was elected to the state senate, became auditor-general of the state, served as state treasurer, and in 1840 was elected to the U.S. Senate. Following his reelection he was appointed treasurer of the U.S. Mint in Philadelphia by President Pierce until he retired from public life in 1858.[17] Of the ninety-nine founding family members resident in the county for whom occupation is known, twenty-three occupied government positions, thirteen in local and ten in state offices.

Social Organization

In her 1826 description of Pittsburgh, a contemporary observer of American life, Mrs. Royall, complained that its society was "graduated and divided with as much regard to rank and dignity as the most scrupulous Hindoos maintain." She yearned for the bygone "days of simple happiness . . . when the unambitious people who were domiciled in the village of 'Fort Pitt,' or the yet unchartered town of Pittsburgh, were ignorant and careless of all the invidious distinctions, which distract and divide the inhabitants of overgrown cities."[18] Her conception of an earlier, seemingly less complicated era is no more accurate than was her view of Pittsburgh as an overgrown city. The determinants of social stratification might change, but some form of social distance existed even in Pittsburgh's earliest days. Like Mrs. Royall, the Bucks were led to believe that "at first there was little differentiation of the population into social classes, except at Pittsburgh, where the army officers made a rather exclusive and homogeneous group."[19] But Robert Harper's examination of the class structure of Western Pennsylvania in the late eighteenth century found great differences in the distribution of wealth which were easily translated into social distinctions. "The new towns that grew up on the western Pennsylvania frontier very early began to demonstrate a class system."[20] Harper suggested that one's position within the class structure was dependent upon wealth, thereby rejecting notions of supposed frontier equality. The uneven distribution of wealth was not restricted to the towns; all the rural townships studied had comparable distributions of wealth, though it was more evenly distributed since the dominant professional and mercantile groups tended to cluster in towns.

Although all the family founders in this study were very successful in their business or professional pursuits, wealth was only one indicator of social status, though an extremely important one. Another was ethnicity. The largest ethnic group, the English, were "first from the standpoint of respectability and significance."[21] By 1820, however, the Scotch-Irish had improved their social and economic position in Allegheny County and throughout the western part of the state. The Denny family genealogy recalls how in Eastern Pennsylvania the Scotch-Irish had been trying to live down a decades-old reputation of being a general nuisance. Indeed, a possible reason why so many chose to settle west of the mountains was that by order of the colony's proprietors, available land in York and Lancaster counties could not be sold to them, and "advantageous offers of removal [should be made] to the Irish settlers . . . in specified townships . . . to remove to Cumberland County."[22] And remove they did. The Bucks estimated that by 1790 they comprised 16 percent of the population of Allegheny and Washington counties.[23] The assimilation of the Scotch-Irish into the larger social fabric in the area enabled the founding families to realize success without the social barriers so familiar to them in the East.

Aside from the English, Scotch-Irish, and Scottish, there were some Welsh, French, Germans, and Swiss in Allegheny County. One observer, writing about 1815, claims that they were "generally friendly" but admits to "various fashions, prejudices and passions in religion and politics."[24] The French, Germans, and Swiss, who did not conform in language or religion, were not universally accepted socially. It was perhaps symbolic that family founder Alexander Negley, from Frankfort, Germany, established himself, not in Pittsburgh, but in rural East Liberty. Descendants of non-German family founders frequently gravitated to Pittsburgh, but his son, Felix Negley (1764–1836), moved still farther away, as indeed many Negleys did, to Tarentum, Pennsylvania.

The earliest social register of sorts was published as a part of the *Honest Man's Almanac* for the years 1812–1813. It listed the names, occupations, and addresses of 148 persons considered by the editors to be prominent citizens, including almost all the founding families living in the city. The criteria used in compiling the list were not stated, and by the editor's own admission the list was not complete.[25]

Organizational membership was yet another indication of one's place in society. The Freemasons were the most prestigious social organization in Pittsburgh. Founded in 1785, "Lodge No. 45 of Ancient York Masons included on its roll the names of the town's leading citizens."[26] While both Episcopalians, especially the old military officers of the Revolution, and Presbyterians belonged, Lodge 45 was partly religious in nature. It maintained a rather close alliance with the Presbyterian church.[27] Those not desiring membership in Lodge 45 could join an Ohio-based lodge which also held its meetings in Pittsburgh, or one of the two chapters of the Knights Templar. No tensions seemed to have existed among the various masonic organizations nor could any significant stratification be found, as some individuals belonged to both lodges at once. Founding family members could be found in all four societies.

In the second decade of the nineteenth century a spate of new organizations were founded, ostensibly to advance one or another worthy cause, perhaps in the "noblesse oblige" tradition. The Pittsburgh Humane Society, established in 1813, had as its expressed objective to "alleviate the distresses of the poor—to supply the wants of the hungry, the naked and the aged—to administer comfort to the widow, the orphan and the sick."[28] All this was to be accomplished on dues of $2.00 a year! Family founders Rev. Francis Herron and Benjamin Bakewell were ward committeemen in the society.

The Pittsburgh Permanent Library Company (1813) required an initial contribution of $10.00 and dues of $5.00 per year. Since only members could borrow books, participation was effectively restricted to polite society. Despite its private membership, the library was quartered in the courthouse, a building built and maintained with public funds. Subscribers were encouraged to deposit their private book collections with the company. It is difficult to imagine how this practice could have avoided becoming a matter of prestige among the members. Their scholarly enthusiasm was questionable, as the library was open only on Saturday evenings. Rev. Francis Herron served as president with Benjamin Page, manager, and Benjamin Bakewell, a director.

Younger members of "respectable society" desirous of more active pursuits had two fire companies from which to choose, the Eagle (1810) or the Vigilant (1811). Of the two, the Eagle was more exclusive; admission "was guarded with the precautions of a social club."[29] In order for a candidate to gain entrance, the unanimous agreement of the membership was required. In 1816 yet another fire company, the Neptune, was founded, the social origins of which remain obscure. William Eichbaum, Jr., son-in-law of family founder John Johnston, was an engineer of the Eagle. The Liggetts were members of the Vigilant.

Students of scripture who could afford the $50.00 life membership fee or $2.00 per year might join the Pittsburgh Bible Society. Among its twelve officers were seven ministers representing the various forms of Presbyterianism. Rev. Francis Herron was the recording secretary; Benjamin Page served as a director.

Spawned by a popular interest in natural science, the Pittsburgh Chemical and Physiological Society (1813) was founded "by a number of scientific gentlemen." Like the library company, it occupied a room in the courthouse. A library, chemical apparatus, and "a valuable cabinet of mineralogy" suggest its activities. Ebenezer Denny's son Harmer was the secretary of this society during this period.

Since American society was in a state of rapid change at this time, it is difficult to determine any rank order in which these organizations may have been arranged. Moreover, a number of persons were officers in two or more organizations, indicating a lack of any exclusive social stratification within the elite. Despite this fluidity, some organizations plainly were more prestigious than others, as in the case of the fire companies, whose memberships were not interlocking.[30] It is possible, though, to construct some hierarchical outline for these organizations without attaching great significance to the extent to which membership in any given organization indicated one's social position. Such a hierarchy is presented in figure 3.

Religion

The development of a local religious social structure antedated the establishment of the various congregations. Though the class distinctions which were later to characterize the denominations had not fully emerged, a sense of religious identification was always strong. While it may be argued that two and one-half centuries after the Protestant Reformation, the various religions on the American frontier

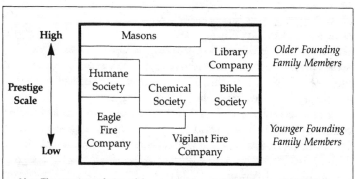

Note: The prestige ordering of the organizations in this figure was derived from the occupational backgrounds of the officers of each organization as listed elsewhere in *The Pittsburgh Directory for 1815.*

FIGURE 3. **Prestige Ordering of Organizations Listed in the** *Pittsburgh Directory for 1815.*

found themselves doctrinally ill-defined, it was partly true that "Protestantism in the early days signified little more than a stout opposition to Roman Catholicism."[31] The numerous Presbyterian denominations, whose adherents may have been unsure of the supposed theological questions originally dividing them or even precisely what they themselves stood for, were quite clear about what was not acceptable. "The Presbyterians, who constituted the bulk of the English-speaking Protestants, had looked askance when the Episcopalians, whom they regarded as closely akin to Roman Catholics, formed their church organization."[32]

The Presbyterians registered even greater shock when Methodist preachers came to Pittsburgh. Methodism had promised salvation to all who believed and obeyed, but with limited success, "for prejudice, bigotry, and sensuality had so effectually enchained and blinded the minds of the inhabitants that it was called 'A Sodom in miniature.' "[33] The Presbyterians had erected a church as early as 1786, but after seven years its pastorate had fallen vacant and the church was closed. When John Wrenshall, a family founder commonly referred to as the Father of Methodism in Pittsburgh, arrived in 1796, he was permitted use of the church. After a few Sundays of preaching attended by successively larger audiences, he found the church padlocked and was notified that it was no longer at his disposal. Despite the fact that they held no services themselves, the Presbyterians would not permit the use of their building by adherents of the new sect of Methodists whom they called "the offspring of the devil."[34]

The Old World antagonisms based upon theological differences were far from dead in Pittsburgh, and increasingly they were reinforced by ethnic considerations. Gradually, ethnic distinctions came to mean social class distinctions.[35] An example of this occurred in 1815. The recently founded Pittsburgh Humane Society involved a modicum of interchurch cooperation in that seven ministers representing a number of churches sat together on the board of directors. Excluded, however, were clergymen from the Catholic, Lutheran, and Covenanter churches. The reasons for excluding Catholics (who were mainly Irish) and Lutherans (who were mainly Germans and Swiss) certainly followed ethnic lines since both groups were socially isolated. The German Lutherans even maintained their own school taught by their pastor.[36] Irish and even English Catholics were denied full participation in American life until well into the twentieth century. The case of the Covenanters is noteworthy since they were Scotch-Irish and a splinter group of Presbyterianism, a religion long-plagued by schisms. But unlike the First and Second Presbyterian Churches in Pittsburgh, they were a sect, lower-class and doctrinally strict. To the clergymen of the Pittsburgh Humane Society, they were socially unacceptable. Like the Catholics and Lutherans, Covenanters were not of their class.[37]

It is possible to construct a religiously based social hierarchy for Pittsburgh in 1820 because only eight churches existed at the time and a few complete name lists are available, as is some anecdotal information. The First Presbyterian Church was the oldest church in Pittsburgh and enjoyed the largest membership. Under the lengthy pastorate (1811–1850) of a family founder, Rev. Francis Herron, the congregation recovered from the schism of 1804, which had resulted in the formation of the Second Presbyterian Church. (It was to suffer yet another in 1833 with the New School formation of the Third Presbyterian Church.) Presbyterianism in Pittsburgh might have been fractionalized, but it was dominant especially in terms of numbers, thus its values largely dictated what attitudes the city held. It was also culturally dominant over most of the rural hinterland.[38]

The Episcopalians, accustomed to social dominance in many other parts of the United States, were not dismayed, threatened, and certainly not converted by the Presbyterians. Although the Episcopalians were plagued by financial woes and an inability to keep a pastor, they claimed a large portion of the city's most respected citizens and most of the old military elite. Germans who desired accceptance into the mainstream of society generally had converted to some form of Presbyterianism, but the Episcopalians were not without some attractions of their own. The English Lutherans, themselves without a church, were annoyed that many of their most substantial families had been "diverted from their spiritual mother" and joined the Episcopal church, choosing Episcopalianism presumably because of "the close resemblance in doctrine and usage of their own Church."[39] This author seems unaware of the increased prestige and participation in public life attendant to membership in the Episcopal church.

The Methodists, who were mostly English, established a church in 1810. Their congregation was conspicuous for its lack of notable members. Moreover, they attempted to increase their numbers by offering sermons in German. This may not have been opprobrious to their English-speaking rivals, but the Germans, together with the Irish Catholics and Covenanters, were so low on the social scale that their inclusion did little for the social elevation of the Methodists as a whole.[40] Although a German Lutheran church existed in the city, there is no evidence that either the Fahnestock or Anshutz families were members.

Lowest in prestige as well as numbers were the Roman Catholics. After the French evacuation of Fort Duquesne in 1758, the few Catholic families in the area were dependent upon itinerant missionaries. Half a century was to elapse before they received a resident pastor. He at once devoted himself to the construction of a church, lending visibility to an otherwise unnoticed denomination. In 1820 the Catholics in the entire Pittsburgh area numbered fewer than three hundred. Their numbers had suffered attrition from Protestant and especially Presbyterian proselytization. Family founder John Johnston's biography gives an interesting anecdote in this regard: "With Ebenezer Denny's co-operation he established in 1809 a Sabbath school in the courthouse on Market Street. It was solely for the benefit of the poor, particularly for the children of Roman Catholic families who were found running at large on the streets."[41] The story, incidentally, also indicates the political clout of family founders who were able to use public property for sectarian purposes under the pretense of improving poor social conditions allegedly existing among Catholics.

It has been argued that in a society at this stage of development, religious affiliation did not carry the weight in determining social distinctions which it was later to assume. Among the various Protestant denominations that may well hold true, for the gulf separating them from the Roman Catholic church was probably far greater than the social distance between any two Protestant churches.

The gulf could be crossed only if one were willing to shed one's Catholicism. So it was with the French-born Felix Brunot, who was able to become Pittsburgh's most respected physician only after he had removed a stumbling block by converting to the Episcopal church. By the same token, severe penalties could befall those who embraced Catholicism. Reuben Sturgeon (1783–1832), son of strict rural Presbyterian parents, was disinherited by his father upon his marriage to a Catholic and his subsequent conversion to that faith. After his ostracism by the Sturgeon family, Reuben moved his family to Ohio where he and his children faded into oblivion. Significantly, Reuben was the only founding family member to become a Catholic in the 1820 period.

In this period, religious affiliation is known for fifty-seven founding family members age seventeen and over. Of this adult group the great bulk, 68 percent, were Presbyterians, but only one belonged to the Covenanter sect. Partly because they were so numerous and partly because they had improved their lot substantially from what they had known in Eastern Pennsylvania, the Presbyterians were able to make theirs the most prestigious religion in Allegheny County.

The second most prominent denomination, both in terms of prestige and popularity among the founding families, was the Episcopal church. About 18 percent of the founding family members were adherents, but they counted among their number many of Pittsburgh's most substantial and influential citizens. While the Episcopalians were concentrated in Pittsburgh, the Presbyterians were dominant in both the county's rural areas as well as in Pittsburgh.

Few founding family members belonged to the remaining churches. The Methodists, 7 percent, composed mostly of the

Wrenshall family; the German Lutherans, 4 percent, mostly Negleys; and one Catholic, the maverick Reuben Sturgeon, together accounted for a mere 12 percent of the total.

Figure 4 attempts to reconstruct the religious social structure of Pittsburgh about 1820. The size of the areas designating each denomination is roughly comparable to its membership. The position and configuration of each area indicate its relative social standing. It is not intended as a definitive statement, nor should it be assumed that one's religious affiliation was necessarily synonomous with one's position within the general social structure. (See also table 29 below.)

The values held by the Protestant churches, and primarily the Presbyterians, became the standard for public morals, but their attitudes regarding prohibition, gambling, sabbatarianism, dancing, and theatrical entertainment were destined for grave revision over the course of the nineteenth century. One of the most dramatic changes in attitude concerned prohibition. Around 1820, tavernkeeping and the selling of liquor were of such respectability that many of the most esteemed citizens had practiced these occupations. Others distilled whiskey or brewed beer. Their ranks included elders of the church and public officials. No laws prohibited Sunday liquor sales.

The initial impetus toward temperance reform came from the prestigious Masons to which most of Pittsburgh's leading citizens belonged. Their meetings, traditionally held in the taverns, "had been conducive of almost everything except sobriety." It had been an embarrassment, but in 1810 the removal of the lodge to rented quarters was a simple although effective expedient in removing the "temptation to excessive drinking."[42]

If dealing in liquor carried no stigma, neither did gambling. As early as 1798 the borough of Pittsburgh was permitted by the Pennsylvania state legislature to conduct a lottery for the construction of piers to defend its eroding riverbanks. Even churches were erected by means of a lottery—Trinity Episcopal in 1805 and the First Presbyterian in 1808.[43]

All the religious denominations were united in their oppo-

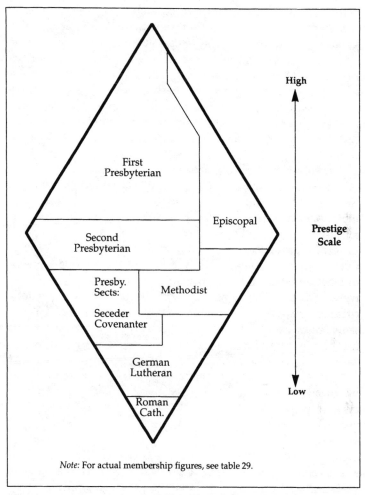

High

Prestige
Scale

Low

Note: For actual membership figures, see table 29.

FIGURE 4. **Religious Structure of Pittsburgh in 1820**

sition to avoidable work on Sunday. But most churches frowned upon dancing on any day of the week. Those who violated the code "were sometimes given public notice of suspension from Communion for this fault."[44] The churches experienced difficulty in enforcing the injunction when the leading citizens refused to obey. The Nevilles, the most socially prominent founding family, did dance, "and had their sons taught by dancing masters. With the gentlemen in town thus favoring the art, others were bound to follow their social lead."[45]

Thwarted in their effort at exercising effective social control, the churches were not reluctant to call upon government to uphold their values. The Presbyterian church, still recovering from memories of English Restoration drama, was adamantly opposed to the theater. In 1804 it induced Pittsburgh to place a prohibitive tax on theatrical entertainment. Despite the tax and the disapproval of powerful religious leaders, Pittsburgh "was in many ways the best theatre town in the new country [the Ohio Valley]." It had several amateur theater organizations, one of which consisted entirely of lawyers. The theater occupying a part of the courthouse moved into its own building in 1812. Despite the support of the *Pittsburgh Gazette*, opposition persisted and the theater went out of business when hard times came in 1819.[46] No record could be found of any founding family involvement with a theatrical enterprise.

Conclusion

The purpose of this chapter is to place the founding families within the total society in Pittsburgh and Allegheny County in 1820 and to demonstrate that they were among the area's socially prominent and economically privileged citizens. It is not necessary that they either constituted the entirety of the local upper class, nor that they were at the extreme pinnacle of power and prestige, but only that they were within the local upper class in this early period.

Because of this, the group could not be expected to conform to the larger society in terms of age structure, ethnicity, occupational distribution, participation in government, membership in social organizations, religious affiliation, or even adherence to social mores. It is precisely this lack of similarity to the general population that underscores their distinct social standing. Some areas of distinction were obviously more important than others. Of all the variables mentioned above, the most important was occupation. It was in this critical dimension that the founding families enjoyed a most favored position, economically and therefore socially, because the upper class in 1820 was primarily predicated on wealth. While many of the variables tended to be interdependent, some, such as rank in the military and the holding of government office, often enhanced one's social position without being interdependent upon a primary occupation. Thus, John Johnston's position as a postmaster of Pittsburgh had little effect on his wire manufacturing business.

Society was in far greater agreement concerning the prestige accorded each occupation and the social position of its holder, than it was regarding ethnicity, religious affiliation, or organizational membership. Society was still in a state of rapid transition, leaving the finer aspects of ethnic identification and institutional membership to succeeding generations to define. At this time it caused no consternation when in 1814 the foreign-born German, William Eichbaum (1787–1866), married Rebecca Johnston, whose father was a trustee of the Presbyterian church. Nor was it found peculiar when the famed glass manufacturer, Benjamin Bakewell, concurrently supported both the Presbyterian and Unitarian churches.[47] It was at once symbolic of the age and paradoxical that "many non-Catholics contributed liberally towards it," when the Roman Catholics began building a new church in 1827.[48]

Yet all this is not to say that confusion reigned. Some religious and ethnic groups were unquestionably more prestigious than others, but an excessive amount of importance must not be attached to this. True, the bulk of the founding family members conformed to one another in terms of ethnicity and religion, but, as in the case of the Negleys, it was possible to contravene them and still be upper class. Despite his German birth and membership in the First German United Evangelical Church, of which he was a founder, Alexander Negley was socially prominent. His ownership of most of East Liberty and his grist and fulling mills placed him in the economic elite, and therefore, the social elite of the 1820s. His ethnicity and religion certainly did not aid him in his ascent, but neither did they disqualify him.

Though many founding family members belonged to prestigious societies and religious bodies, many did not. The families in this formative period were still socially heterogeneous, partly reflecting the heterogeneity of the larger society. Fourteen percent had a non-English-speaking background, and some of these still belonged to a non-English-speaking church. It was the descendants of the family founders who would define the social order with greater precision. The occupationally successful among them would become increasingly homogeneous in character even as the population of Pittsburgh and Allegheny County became more diverse or heterogeneous in every respect.

V

Occupation

Vertical Mobility/Stability

A FUNDAMENTAL CONSIDERATION in tracing succeeding generations from the family founders is the nature and extent of vertical occupational mobility and its changing patterns in the nineteenth century. Although social mobility is not always a direct function of occupational mobility, it is nonetheless recognized that occupation is and has been associated with income, education, and community reputation, all of which tend to relate to one another and to identify with position within the social structure. Since it has been established that initially all the founding family members were within the upper class, though not necessarily at the very top, most of the vertical occupational mobility that did occur was downward. Some did become truly eminent, surpassing even that position established by the family founder, but even in such instances, it will not be interpreted as movement to a higher class, since their ancestors were already upper class.

It is recognized that in America the terms *elite* and *upper class* have referred to different but not entirely unrelated concepts. Both designate a high position, but *elite* indicates occupational position whereas *upper class* indicates social position. Although both the elite and the upper class normally realize a high income, the elite derive it from their occupation, while the upper class is thought to receive it from inherited wealth. They are, however, related in other ways that tend to make the two less easily separated. Throughout American history, descendants of the elite have been assimilated into the upper class in two or three generations. It is impossible to determine at what point this occurs, if indeed there is any given point in a process so gradual. It is also true that the elite and the upper class overlap, and to a very considerable degree. Many members of the upper class are, and always have been, elite as well. For the purposes of this study, these two aspects will be combined into the single term, *elite upper class,* thus eliminating the need to differentiate the two parts of what is here used as a more comprehensive term. The term then is used to designate in a general way those who occupy a high position within the socioeconomic structure.[1]

The degree of occupational success will be divided into three categories: successful, marginal, and unsuccessful. The first category includes all those who maintained their position within the elite upper class. In this group are almost all the professionals, manufacturers, bankers, business executives, military men of high rank, government officials in an executive capacity, and demonstrably successful merchants and farmers.

Of the several factors used to determine an individual's success category, one is the number of occupations pursued concurrently. Occupational concurrence was especially prevalent among those engaged in commerce or agriculture. A merchant, for example, who not only retailed his goods but imported them, sold to other merchants, and speculated in land and coal rights on the side, was decidedly above the storekeeper who only kept shop. The same pertains to a farmer who added more land to his holdings, possibly rented out portions of his land, erected a gristmill, and was a justice of the peace as well. The pursuance of concurrent occupations related or unrelated to the central one, was a key indicator in the decision to place a founding family member in the successful category.

Similarly, the absence of outside interests was a factor in defining the marginally successful. This classification embraces those whose status appears materially below that of the successful. Included here are the small merchants and farmers without outside interests, clerks and bookkeepers, and officers in the military below the rank of captain.

The lowest group, the unsuccessful, consists of those who declined in occupational status to a middle-class position and, in the instance of three laborers, what appears to be a lower-class position. Also in this group are mechanics, foremen, and privates in the military. If a person's job title was vague, other known characteristics were evaluated in order to place him in the correct category.

This study encompasses 1,006 founding family members, but occupational data on 397 of them has not been used in assessing maintenance of position from that achieved by the family founders, leaving a total of 609. Several groups were eliminated. The family founders themselves have been eliminated since their success was the standard to which all subsequent generations were compared. Married women were excluded because at this time in history their socioeconomic positions rested largely on the success of their husbands. Unmarried women who had no careers were excluded; those who pursued independent careers were retained. Men who died young through war, accident, or illness and were unable to establish a full career were also deleted. Finally, those whose occupational histories are unknown had to be eliminated.

Occupational success in this study is considered on an intergenerational basis, that is, from father to son. Success is measured in the ability to launch the next generation from a position of advantage. Therefore, once the baton has been passed to the children, subsequent economic reverses need not seriously affect the determinants in ascertaining career success. For example, if a father were financially ruined at age sixty, after an otherwise successful career, he is considered a success, especially if his children were raised with the advantages needed to establish their own careers. It should be noted that such instances were rare. General patterns of success or failure tended to characterize an entire career.

Table 6 shows that, of the 609 founding family members for whom occupational data was tabulated, 151 (25 percent) held jobs in the marginally successful or unsuccessful occupation category, whereas the overwhelming majority, 75 percent, maintained their position within the elite upper class. In other words, almost one in four was unable to maintain his or her position in the elite upper class, but very few could be characterized as unsuccessful.

Not only were the founding families largely successful, but this rate of success was sustained throughout the nineteenth and early twentieth centuries. Table 7, which subdivides the above table by date of birth, shows how stable the group was.

Changes in the proportion which the successful formed as a part of the whole were very slight. Its percentage of the total

TABLE 6
Occupational Success Rates (N=609)

Successful	Marginal	Unsuccessful	Declined[a]
75% (458)	19% (113)	6% (38)	25% (151)

a. Declined = Marginal + Unsuccessful

TABLE 7
Occupational Success Rates by Date of Birth (N=609)

Born	Successful		Marginal		Unsuccessful	
Before 1820	77%	(141)	18%	(33)	5%	(9)
1820–1839	76	(96)	21	(27)	3	(4)
1840–1859	74	(131)	17	(29)	9	(16)
After 1860	73	(90)	20	(24)	7	(9)
Total		(458)		(113)		(38)

never varied more than 1.5 percent from one time period to the next and changed less than 4 percent from the earliest to the last time period. An exceedingly slow decline in the percentage of successful did occur, however, which seems upon first observation to be at variance with theories advanced by Baltzell, Pessen, and others. These theories support the idea that by the late nineteenth century the American upper class had matured into a true upper class, developing a consciousness of its own identity as manifested in social registers, exclusive clubs, upper-class neighborhoods, and so forth. This consciousness should have theoretically resulted in a more efficient operation of the accumulation of advantages, which would have prevented downward social mobility. If these theories hold true, a higher percentage should be maintained within the ranks of the successful. Since this is not true of the founding families, either a new theory must be devised or the data must be reinterpreted.

The above data include all the founding family members (with the exceptions noted). If the non-core husbands and the children of founding family daughters are excluded, leaving a core group of 317, a different result is obtained (table 8). Purged of "outside" influences possibly biasing the data (such as the ability of the women to select successful husbands[2]), the figures tend to lend credence to the theories on maintenance within the elite, but with a slight variation. As before, the successful first generation was followed by two equally

TABLE 8
Core Group Occupational Success Rates by Date of Birth (N=317)

Born	Successful		Marginal		Unsuccess-ful	
Before 1819	75%	(83)	21%	(23)	4%	(5)
1820–1839	72	(49)	25	(17)	3	(2)
1840–1859	73	(59)	17	(14)	10	(8)
After 1860	77	(44)	11	(6)	12	(7)
Total		(235)		(60)		(22)

successful generations. (The post-1860 group were the most successful due, in part, to the social forces described earlier.) But a change of some significance occurs within the marginal and unsuccessful groups. As an inverse proportion of the successful group, the percentage of marginals correspondingly declines after the second generation; that is, as more core members are successful, fewer hold marginal positions. However, the percentage of the unsuccessful increases significantly in the groups born after 1839, eventually exceeding even that of the marginally successful group.

Previously it was stated that over the four time periods, the percentage changes experienced by the successful were very slight. While this is certainly true when observing aggregate statistics, it may well be that a considerable amount of shifting occurred from one time period to the next among the successful, marginal, and unsuccessful. If this is true, then it would hardly substantiate theories which suppose stability within the elite upper class. What must be determined is the percentage of successful children who were also descended from successful parents. Excluding the family founders (24), only 39 of the 434 successful (core and non-core) were children of marginal or unsuccessful parents. This represents only 9 percent of the total number of successful. Even when the number of successful children whose parents' occupational success is unknown is deducted (26), the number of successful who were children of successful parents is 364 (85 percent). Not including those whose rank is unknown, the percentage of successful whose parents were also successful is 90 percent. Since it is doubtful that all the unknown were marginal or unsuccessful, the actual percentage of successful children having successful parents was between 85 and 90 percent of the total. It can be said with justification that, over the four time periods, a very great amount of stability existed in the successful group.

If success begets success, the same may hold true for the marginal and the unsuccessful. Of the 151 persons in these two categories, 44 (29 percent) had parents who were also either marginal or unsuccessful. An additional 6 percent were children of parents whose success category is unknown. Therefore, between 29 and 35 percent of the marginal or unsuccessful were children of parents who had declined in occupational status. If this percentage seems small, it should be noted that the chances of this occurring randomly were below 25 percent since the entirety of the first generation was successful. Because the successful dominated the earlier periods to an even greater degree than they did the later ones, and those who declined were correspondingly distributed in the later periods, the possibility of a marginal or unsuccessful child succeeding a marginal or unsuccessful parent was increased. Therefore, a parent who was downwardly mobile did tend to condemn his children to the same fate.

The fact that such a large percentage of the last age group, those born after 1859, fell into the unsuccessful category does not refute the theory that the late-nineteenth-century consciousness of kind, coupled with the accumulation of advantages, prevented downward mobility. About one-third of those who were unsuccessful had a father who was also classified either as unsuccessful or as only marginally successful. If the accumulation of advantages maintained the successful, it cannot be expected to lift those beyond its field of effect who were outside the supposed upper-class consciousness of kind.

It is not intended that occupational stability across generations be emphasized to the point of ignoring such movement that did occur both up and down. The percentage of those children of a marginal or unsuccessful parent who realized their own main chance and were able to climb once again to the successful category, although not very great, was not negligible. Those who rose again from marginal or unsuccessful parents comprised, depending on the time period, anywhere from 9.1 to 9.7 percent of the successful category. The 25 percent of the total group for whom information is known who declined from the occupational category of the family founder is more significant. The main point remains that the founding families were, to a very large degree, able to maintain themselves within the elite upper class.

Occupational Distribution

A discussion of occupational success should rightly begin with an examination of the various occupations themselves. As a group, the founding families pursued a wide variety of occupations; many individuals engaged in several concurrent occupations during their careers. Almost one-half held two or more occupations at once. Sixteen percent of those for whom such information is available held two occupations at once, 5.9 percent held three, 1.5 percent held four, 1.1 percent held five, and 0.7 percent held six. None of those holding two or more jobs at once were ranked as marginally successful or unsuccessful. Indeed, as a rule, those holding two or more positions were of exceptionally high social status. Even more prevalent was the practice of pursuing two or more occupations successively. Of the 657 whose occupations (but not necessarily success categories) are known, some 318 or almost one-half went on to pursue a second occupation. Of those who held two positions previously, 171 (54 percent) went on to pursue a third. The number of persons holding jobs and the number of jobs they held is shown in figure 5. The pattern of a 50 percent decline for each additional occupation is consistent, even to the sixth occupation. Self-advancement was undoubtedly a major motive for holding so many positions. Additional light will be shed on multiple occupations in a later discussion of family firms.

The founding families pursued a variety of occupations. Table 9 shows in greater detail how occupations were distributed and the extent to which each was pursued, listing only the last, and generally most prestigious, occupation. Excluding 27 women who were either unemployed or were identified as philanthropists, some forty-six different occupations are listed. The average number of individuals in a single occupation is 13.4, or 2 percent of the total. While the most popular occupation was farmer, this comprised less than 6.5 percent of the total. The founding family occupations were so widely distributed that only three other occupations, lawyer, banker, and military officer, comprised more than 5 percent of the total.

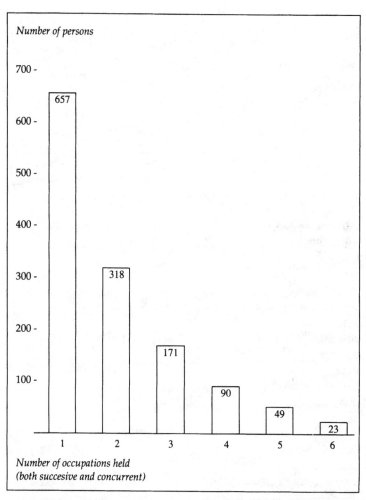

FIGURE 5. Number of Persons by Number of Occupations Held

More helpful than a simple chart showing the occupational distribution for the entire period is one that shows change within the distribution. In table 10 the occupations have been collapsed into twelve associated groups, showing the extent to which each was pursued in 1820, 1860, and 1900. It reveals a

TABLE 9
Occupational Distribution of the Founding Families (N=618)

Occupation	No.	%
Professional		
Judge	9	1.5
Lawyer	31	5.0
Doctor	23	3.7
Clergyman	25	4.0
Editor/author	12	1.9
Teacher/professor	17	2.8
Engineer	17	2.8
Scientist	2	0.3
Commercial		
Banker	35	5.7
Merchant	20	3.2
Commission merchant	4	0.7
Shipper/wholesaler	15	2.4
Dry goods merchant	3	0.5
Broker	10	1.6
Real estate/insurance dealer	25	4.0
Agent/manager	24	3.9
Store owner	13	2.1
Druggist	3	0.5
Hotel owner	3	0.5
President	21	3.4
Secretary/treasurer	23	3.7
Production (entrepreneurial)		
Manufacturer (unspecified)	14	2.3
Iron manufacturer	15	2.4
Glass manufacturer	7	1.1
Food/product processor	18	2.9
Printer	5	0.8
Builder/contractor	5	0.8
Mine owner/operator	6	1.0
Refinery owner/operator	5	0.8
Clerical/Mechanical		
Bookkeeper	4	0.7
Clerk	14	2.3
Mechanic	14	2.3
Laborer	3	0.5
Foreman	1	0.2

Occupation	No.	%
Farming/Landholding		
Farmer	40	6.5
Landowner	28	4.5
Government		
Federal/state official	22	3.6
Local official (executive)	21	3.4
Local official	13	2.1
Military		
General	2	0.3
Colonel	10	1.6
Major	16	2.6
Captain	10	1.6
1st Lieutenant	2	0.3
2nd Lieutenant	3	0.5
Private	5	0.8

significant amount of shifting in almost all categories; some occupations constantly gaining in numbers, others losing, and still others gaining and then losing. None, however, lost and then gained. The most significant increase occurred in finance and related occupations. This paralleled the increased importance of the organizational sector of the American economy: in 1900 more than one out of five founding family members were in the financial field (bankers, brokers, and so forth), triple the number in 1820. Yet even in 1820 the professions had attracted more than twice as many as the financial sector and continued to exceed it in every time period.

Increases followed by decline in both the military and the clergy should not be surprising, but for manufacturing, a 6 percent increase followed by a 5 percent decline requires some explanation. The careers of founding family members engaged in manufacturing reveal a pattern whereby their firms were either forced out of business or, more commonly, absorbed by much larger enterprises. Founding family members often received a position with the new company, presumably as a part of previously negotiated arrangements.

TABLE 10
Change in Occupational Distribution, 1820–1900

Occupation	1820 (N=111)		1860 (N=244)		1900 (N=263)		% change, 1820–1900
Professional	11.7%	(13)	15.1%	(37)	23.1%	(61)	+11.4
Clergyman	2.7	(3)	7.0	(17)	2.0	(5)	− 0.7
Banker/broker/ insurance	5.4	(6)	13.1	(32)	21.3	(56)	+15.9
Business executive	0.9	(1)	4.1	(10)	12.5	(33)	+11.6
Manufacturing/ construction	7.2	(8)	13.5	(33)	8.8	(23)	+ 1.6
Mining/ refining	0.9	(1)	1.2	(3)	2.7	(7)	+ 1.8
Merchant	11.7	(13)	7.8	(19)	3.8	(10)	− 7.9
Keepers (store, etc.)	4.5	(5)	2.0	(5)	3.4	(9)	− 0.7
Government official	15.3	(17)	9.8	(24)	5.7	(15)	− 9.6
Clerk/ laborer, etc.	2.7	(3)	4.1	(10)	8.8	(23)	+ 6.1
Military	10.8	(12)	11.1	(27)	3.4	(9)	− 7.4
Agriculture	26.1	(29)	11.1	(27)	4.5	(12)	−21.6

This happened to the non-core Benjamin F. Brundred (1849–1908), the husband of Elizabeth Dilworth. He owned a one-third share of the Union Refinery in Clarion County, Pennsylvania. He sold his share in the refinery to Standard Oil in return for a position as a manager. His position, incidentally, was more secure in the smaller firm, for when the works which he had sold were abandoned, he lost his job.

Lewis A. Anshutz (1863–1937) was somewhat more fortunate. In addition to being a major stockholder in the Anshutz Company, a stove manufacturer, he was secretary and treasurer of the firm. In the late 1890s he sold his shares to the peculiarly named Pittsburgh Stove and Range Company of Springfield, Massachusetts. As compensation for his shares, he received a position with the Massachusetts Life Insurance Company.

Instances such as these account for at least a part of the increase in the business executive category. I am not suggesting that this increase was a direct function of the decline in the manufacturing sector. The 4.5 percentage point loss experienced by manufacturing was more than compensated for by an 8.5 percentage point increase in the business executive sector. The concurrent increase and decrease in these two categories after 1860 bear some relationship to one another, but not a direct one. The increasing popularity of executive careers among the founding families reflected trends in the economy already in progress by 1860.

This is true of other occupations as well. The Civil War, a symbolic watershed in American history, was not an occupational watershed in any tangible sense and did not radically alter the direction of the economy. During the antebellum industrialization of the United States, the founding families increased their participation in manufacturing and construction, with a corresponding decline in agricultural and mercantile pursuits. These older occupations, associated with preindustrial societies, were gradually replaced by more dynamic opportunities in an industrially-based economy. Indeed, landholding (though it can hardly be described as a typical founding family occupation) was the ultimate in passivity and dependence on outside forces. It did not create its own good fortune; rather it waited inertly for an increasing population to drive up land values. Its nearest comparative, agriculture, was not nearly so static. But even agriculture, while it may have once afforded a relatively secure place in the occupational hierarchy, lost ground relative to the more lucrative rewards afforded by business and industry. In addition, the lands held near Pittsburgh were sold and the monies invested in urban-oriented ventures. The locally-based commission merchant, an independent entrepreneur, was rendered obsolete by large-scale systems of marketing and distribution. Likewise the military, with its attendant battlefield glories and honor, however chimerical, held little attraction in the period of comparative peace following the Civil War. Sensing many of these changes, the founding families were not hesitant to abandon less profitable careers in search of new opportunities. In a very real sense, these succeeding generations carried on in the tradition of the family founders.

Founding family members who moved into the business sector did so at considerable risk, especially in view of the periodic panics and depressions that accompanied American economic growth. Those who were successful possessed foresight and experienced good fortune, since financial opportunity could easily end in financial ruin. They were bold leaders in the organization of industries, railroads, and banking establishments. But to stay on top, they could not be sentimental. Joseph Dilworth (1826–1885), for example, was one of the organizers and a director of the Northern Pacific Railroad. He might have fallen victim to the Panic of 1873, but he had had the foresight to accept tracts of land in Minnesota in lieu of railroad stock. When the Northern Pacific was forced into bankruptcy, his properties remained in hand.

At this point it may be profitable to compare the occupational changes within the founding families to those in the total American work force. Occupational classification changed so radically in the 1800s that comparing one census to another is rather difficult; even more difficult is comparing the percentages of the various occupations to those of the founding families. Despite the unsatisfactory nature of the data, some comparison can be made. Table 11 expresses in percentages those employed in the various occupational categories as adapted from the census. Although more specific, the founding family data were arranged to correspond to the census data. The occupational profile of the U.S. population should not be expected to resemble that of the founding families. However, significant increases or decreases in a given occupation should be reflected to some degree within the founding families.

The percentage of the U.S. population engaged in agriculture fell by almost a half in the eighty years after 1820, and the founding families, who were not nearly as committed to agriculture initially, also abandoned this occupation. Conversely, the percentage of the U.S. population in the professions, ser-

TABLE 11
Occupational Distribution of the United States and the Founding Families,
1820–1900 (%)

	1820		1860		1900	
Occupation	U.S.	Founding Families	U.S.	Founding Families	U.S.	Founding Families
Agriculture	71.9	26.1	59.5	11.1	37.5	4.5
Mining	—	—	1.6	1.2	2.6	2.7
Manufacturing, hand trades, construction	12.1	10.8	18.3	21.7	27.5	30.1
Transportation, trade, finance, real estate	—	—	7.4	22.9	16.7	28.5
Professional, service, government	—	—	12.4	31.9	14.3	30.8
Not allocated	16.0	63.1	.8	11.2	1.3	3.4

Source: Percentage of the U.S. work force in each occupation derived from: U.S. Bureau of the Census, *Historical Statistics of the United States* (Washington, D.C.: Government Printing Office, 1960), p. 74. Agricultural statistics include forestry and fishing.

vice industries, and government increased, but the percentage of the founding families in those occupations actually decreased slightly: they had entered those occupations in advance of the general population. In other words, the founding families had anticipated the various changes which the U.S. population later experienced.

Although the occupational profile of the founding families is not proportional to that of the United States, it is interesting to note that it conforms increasingly with the passing of each time period. In 1820 the average percentage difference of each occupation category listed between the United States and the founding families was 31 percent. By 1860 this difference had been reduced to 16 percent, and by 1900 it was down to 11 percent. Increasingly the occupational structure of the United States shifted from the less skilled and locally oriented occupations, especially farming, to the more skilled and specialized occupations such as industry, finance, and the professions, where the founding families were already active.

Business

Of Boston's old upper class, Cleveland Amory writes, "When a family loses its financial stability, it has a way of beginning to disappear."[3] The basis of "financial stability" is normally either wealth, measured in terms of money, securities, land, and so forth, or an income derived from some form of production or commerce, commonly known as business. Since wealth has a habit of dissipating, the pursuit of business, while far from foolproof, has proved itself the more reliable means of maintaining a family in the upper class. In American society, a business career is closely related to economic well-being.

In the first parts of this chapter, occupation was analyzed quantitatively. This and the two sections following discuss occupation in a more particular and somewhat less quantitative sense. I begin with business, which was the mainstay of the founding families. Although the professions, the clergy, and the military are given equal treatment, many of the men in these occupations were to a large extent dependent upon their business relatives, despite the considerable amount of downward occupational mobility within the business sector itself. It was businessmen who amassed such wealth as the founding families did possess—there were no Carnegies, but as early as 1852 Harmer Denny left an estate of $16 to $20 million—and it was they who, in death, willed it to entrepreneur and minister alike.

A more precise distribution of business success rates is presented in table 12. The percentage of those who were successful was remarkably similar from one period to the next, hardly varying at all from the average of 68 percent. Considerable change occurred among those less successful, however. In the first two time periods the greater proportion were in the marginal category, but by the later periods over 40 percent of those who were not successful were in the very lowest success category. Although the number of founding family members in the unsuccessful category increased in the last two time periods, it was not as great an increase as the number who moved from successful to marginal from one genera-

TABLE 12
Success Rates for Businessmen, Founding Family Members by Date of Birth (N=386)

Born	Successful		Marginal		Unsuccess-ful	
Before 1820	68%	(81)	24%	(29)	8%	(9)
1820–1839	67	(46)	29	(20)	4	(3)
1840–1859	67	(85)	20	(25)	13	(16)
After 1859	69	(50)	17	(12)	14	(10)
Total		(262)		(86)		(38)

TABLE 13
Success Rates for Businessmen, Core and Non-Core

	Successful		Marginal		Unsuccess-ful	
Core	70%	(146)	20%	(41)	10%	(22)
Non-Core	66	(116)	25	(45)	9	(16)

tion to the next in the first two time periods. The overall success rate was 75 percent (see table 6), but the rate is lower for those in business (table 13). A comparison of core and non-core businessmen reveals that a slightly greater proportion of the core was unsuccessful, and a considerably larger proportion was successful. What factors explain founding family business success, or lack of it?

In his examination of American business following the Civil War, Alfred D. Chandler has written that the great entrepreneurial achievement of the time was not technological, but organizational: the introduction of the vertically integrated corporation. Stated simply, vertical integration means direct control by a single owner (the corporation) of several or even all phases in the manufacturing of a product, from raw sources to distribution. Chandler adds that "such organizations hardly existed, outside of railroads, before the 1880s."[4]

Among the founding family business enterprises, several instances of vertical integration can be found more than thirty years earlier than Chandler states. In 1818, Samuel R. Johnston (1797–1854) and a partner acquired a printing business. That same year they purchased the *Pittsburgh Gazette*. Besides printing stationery and publishing the newspaper, they also added a bindery and published schools texts and ledgers. These products were sold to the public from a bookstore in Pittsburgh which they owned and operated. In order to insure a steady supply of paper, they erected a papermill in adjacent Beaver County (ca. 1846), and they capped it all with barges to ship the paper products.

A second example is John C. Risher (1815–1889), husband of Nancy McClure, owner and operator of at least one coal mine. On the same land he obtained lumber and built a sawmill which produced timbers for the mine and wood for coal transport barges. By 1851 Risher was transporting his coal and marketing it in Cincinnati, Louisville, and New Orleans. Soon his fleet of barges exceeded his own production capacity and he was able to transport coal from other mines downriver.

Admittedly these sole proprietorships and partnerships of the pre–Civil War founding families were not the large-scale operations of post–Civil War corporations, nor, probably, did they possess a bureaucracy in the modern sense, but the principle of control of the various phases of production was certainly there.

While the founding families were, on occasion, in the vanguard of organizational innovation, they did not neglect technology. Their publications, patents, and other innovative pursuits are too numerous to mention but can be glimpsed in the following partial list.

1775   John Ormsby starts a ferry across the Monongahela River.
1792   George Anshutz builds the first iron furnace in Allegheny County.
1808   Benjamin Bakewell builds the first flint glassworks west of the Alleghenies.
1816   Jacob Negley builds the first steam flour mill west of the Alleghenies.

1821 Samuel R. Johnston begins a sheduled service stagecoach line between Pittsburgh and Philadelphia.

1830 John P. Bakewell receives a patent for a system of glass wheels for clocks.

1833 Samuel R. Johnston builds the first power printing press west of the Alleghenies.

1840s William Eichbaum, husband of Rebecca Johnston, invents a machine to do faint-ruled lettering.
William Eichbaum discovers the secret of manufacturing Russian sheet iron.

1844 Henry Anshutz develops a process for enameling stoves.

1849 Felix Casper Negley organizes a successful speculative gold mining venture to California.

1850s William Eichbaum invents a system of canal locks used in the Sault Sainte Marie ship canal.

1850s Thomas Bakewell establishes the Pittsburgh & Connellsville Railroad Company, earliest in the area, and founds the Pittsburgh Gas Company.

1850 Samuel Fahnestock compiles the first "modern" Pittsburgh city directory.

1857 Benjamin L. Fahnestock erects a white lead works in Pittsburgh for pharmaceutical use, one of the largest in the United States.

1860s Thomas J. Brereton, husband of Amelia Denny, develops a process for distilling oil from coal.

1860 Bakewell, James & Campbell Oil Company is formed by three founding family members one year after Drake's successful well.

1864 Joseph Dilworth is an organizer of the Northern Pacific, a transcontinental railroad.

1864 William Dilworth, Jr., is the first in Pittsburgh to use the Woodworth planing machine.

1865 Francis A. Dilworth attempts to build a gas pipeline to Pittsburgh.

1870 Thomas D. Mellon, husband of Sarah Negley, establishes the banking house of Thomas Mellon & Sons.

1871 John S. Scully, husband of Mary Negley, organizes the First Pool Monongahela Gas Coal Company.

1876 John J. O'Leary, husband of Emma Fahnestock, begins a long-distance pork packing business in St. Paul, Minnesota.

1876 Woodruff McKnight, son of Elizabeth Denny, begins long-distance transportation of oranges in California.

1878   George Senft, husband of Keziah Negley, creates Idlewild Park, to build ridership for the Ligonier Valley Railroad.

1883   Hilary J. Brunot purchases and reorganizes the *Greensburg Daily and Weekly Press.*

1884   Henry P. Burgwin, son of Mary Phillips, moves to Zellwood, Florida, and grows a new species of oranges.

1894   Benjamin F. Brundred, son-in-law of Elizabeth Dilworth, who had spent his career in the oil business, establishes the largest duck farm in Pennsylvania (60,000 per year).

1895   Otis H. Childs, husband of Louise Dilworth, organizes the Lincoln Foundry Company and merges it with United Engineering to improve manufacturing methods.

1899   Stephen Jarvis Adams, husband of Emma Anshutz, holds over one hundred patents in iron manufacturing. He also invents a hand coffee mill, a spring snap, and the Janus-faced clock.

1904   George D. Edwards, husband of Pauline Dilworth, is appointed by the governor of Pennsylvania to codify the state banking laws.

1915   William M. Bakewell establishes the Bakewell Motor Car Company in Pittsburgh.

1915   James M. Fahnestock is cited as the "world's foremost authority on automobile construction" (Society of Automotive Engineers). Author of section on the Model T in *Duke's Auto Encyclopedia.*

These examples are not intended to suggest that all, or even most, founding families built their success on invention or innovation. Indeed, most of the innovations cited were not technologically or economically feasible at that time, and even some of the successful ones encountered social resistance. For example, when William Dilworth (1818–1877) introduced the Woodworth planing machine in 1864, carpenters burned his lumber business, fearful that the machine would replace them. When he rebuilt, they burned it again. The central point here is that a significant portion of the founding family members were willing to take risks by innovating in an effort to achieve success.

Perhaps yet another conclusion may be drawn from the above list. Historians have often asserted that periods of rapid social change and technological development demand different leadership and new talent. The elite upper class, rooted in older values and life-styles, cannot adapt to changing circumstances. Consequently, the descendants of the original elite are replaced by new elite groups. Brooks Adams commented on the social process: "Nothing is commoner than to find families who have been famous in one century sinking into obscurity in the next, not because the children have degenerated, but because fields of activity which afforded the ancestors full scope, have been closed to the offspring."[5] Few would deny that new elites have arisen almost continuously in American society, but it does not necessarily follow that the descendants of elites are continuously "sinking into obscurity" because of some inability to adapt. The parade of inventions, created or borrowed, and business innovations throughout the nineteenth century suggest that the founding families were, in many cases, able not only to keep abreast of the changing economic system but to initiate some of those changes.

In examining the careers of founding family members, it is important to consider where they worked. Of all for whom such information is available, more than one-half were employed at some time in a firm controlled by relatives (called here a family firm). The nature of this employment ranges from "never" to "family firm only" (see table 14). Other career patterns include outside employment before, after, or during their association with the family firm.

TABLE 14
Founding Family Employment Patterns (N=336)

Pattern	%	Number
Never in the family firm	49	166
Outside employment—family firm	6	19
Outside employment—family firm—outside employment	2	8
Family firm—outside employment	8	25
Family firm plus outside interests	13	43
Family firm only	22	75

Each pattern may be interpreted as illustrating a degree or type of dependence upon the family. "Never in the family firm" would seem to indicate the least dependence, and "family firm only," the greatest. "Outside employment—family firm" suggests failure in trying to make one's own way in the world followed by a return home in order to be "maintained" in the elite upper class. "Outside employment—family firm— outside employment" indicates the same thing except that another presumably successful attempt was made to pursue an independent career. "Family firm—outside employment" could indicate that after an initial start given by the family firm, the individual was able to pursue an independent career. Although "family firm only" does not necessarily indicate incompetence or even lack of aggressiveness, "family firm plus outside interests" certainly would indicate a measure of competence and probably more aggressiveness.

The first category is the largest, accounting for almost one-half of the group. Still, 51 percent were at some time during their lives dependent on the family firm. Indeed, 35 percent were employed with a family firm for the entirety of their careers, though more than a third of them pursued outside interests. Those who at one time belonged to a family firm but finished their careers employed elsewhere account for a minor proportion of the total, less than 10 percent. The chances were overwhelming, then, that if a founding family member ever joined a family firm, he would end his career there. Of all those who ever joined a family firm, most did so for life and most had no business interests beyond the family firm.

These proportions remained relatively stable over time, with the exception that by 1900 there was a great increase in family firm employment. The percentage of those who belonged to a family firm and had no outside interests more than doubled while the percentage of those never employed in a family firm fell from 55 to 41 (table 15). By 1900, 59 percent of all founding family members were for some part of their careers connected with a family firm. Individual initiative had indeed given way to dependence.

Some occupational groups within these combined statis-

TABLE 15
Employment Patterns, 1820–1900

Pattern	1820 (N=60)		1860 (N=131)		1900 (N=145)	
Never in the family firm	57%	(34)	55%	(72)	41%	(60)
Outside employment—family firm	5	(3)	6	(7)	6	(9)
Outside employment—family firm—outside employment	2	(1)	2	(3)	3	(4)
Family firm—outside employment	7	(4)	7	(9)	8	(12)
Family firm plus outside interests	15	(9)	15	(20)	10	(14)
Family firm only	15	(9)	15	(20)	32	(46)

TABLE 16
Employment Patterns of Businessmen, 1820–1900

Pattern	1820 (N=23)		1860 (N=56)		1900 (N=76)	
Never in the family firm	35%	(8)	34%	(19)	22%	(17)
Outside employment—family firm	13	(3)	9	(5)	7	(5)
Outside employment—family firm—outside employment	4	(1)	4	(2)	4	(3)
Family firm—outside employment	0	(0)	7	(4)	8	(6)
Family firm plus outside interests	26	(6)	23	(13)	12	(9)
Family firm only	22	(5)	23	(13)	47	(36)

tics showed greater change in dependence on the family firm. The professionals were highly independent in 1820, 71 percent never having belonged to a family firm. By 1860 this had declined to 67 percent, and by 1900 to 61 percent. A similar change occurred in the business sector. Table 16 shows the distribution of those in business: bankers, brokers, insurance agents, business executives, manufacturers, contractors, operators of mines and refineries, merchants, and shopkeepers. The percentage of those who never worked for a family firm declined during the nineteenth century from 35 percent to 22 percent, while the percentage of those employed only by a family firm more than doubled. Those with outside interests declined sharply from 26 percent to 12 percent. This change may reflect factors having nothing to do with competence.

In 1820, given the state of technology, it was both possible and profitable for entrepreneurs, whether employed by a family firm or not, to pursue a variety of business interests. As markets became nationalized, the industries supplying them inevitably became specialized. As a consequence, founding family members pursued fewer business ventures outside the family firm, a trend especially pronounced by the end of the nineteenth century. Moreover, the character of the outside pursuits had changed. Those having multiple interests by 1900 were not as apt to be running two or three unrelated business enterprises. Their pursuits were more likely to be in the form of interlocking directorships.

Family founder John Herron (1792–1863) was involved in a lumbering business, a gristmill, a brickyard, coal mining, and the transportation of coal. His son William A. Herron (1821–1900) also had a full career. By the 1850s, in addition to the family lumber business, he was a partner in a brass foundry, had interests in a cotton batting factory and glassworks, and transported coal by a railroad which he built. Moving into banking, he founded Iron City Trust, Mechanics Bank, and, in 1863, People's Saving Bank. He also owned a real estate business with his two sons. William's son John W. Herron (1851–1910) entered the family real estate business, becoming a partner in 1877. Continuing in this business, he also became vice-president of Commercial National Bank and later president of Commonwealth Trust, which he helped found.

The careers of these three generations of Herrons are typical and illustrate the trend towards specialization and the consequent reduction in the number of unrelated business activities. The first generation seized opportunities wherever they presented themselves, apparently with little attempt to integrate them. The second Herron generation, while still scattering energies over a broad field, began to concentrate on businesses that supported each other. William A. Herron represents a transitional figure in that his early career is similar to his father's, but he attempted to specialize and interrelate his interests later in life. Thus he set a new direction for the third generation. His son's career embraced only the family real estate firm and banking. Outside interests were fewer and less diverse than those of the previous generations. Banking was carefully selected to complement his other business.

This example, typical as it may be, should not obscure the even greater tendency of founding family members either to return to the safety of the family firm after attempting a career elsewhere or never to leave the family firm at all. The percentage whose support was derived only from the family firm was always impressive but grew larger in succeeding generations. And the influence of the family firm, even to those who pursued outside interests all their lives, can scarcely be exaggerated. It provided the initial capital for the more ambitious, and the associations and experience derived from the family firm were of inestimable value in maintaining the founding families within the elite upper class. By 1900 the family firm was the preferred means of securing occupational success.

The statistics that were presented in table 16 showing the degree of dependence on a family firm are probably conservative. A considerably larger percentage of the founding family members were occupationally dependent upon their families without ever having joined a family firm.

The following case illustrates a son's dependence upon his father in a behind-the-scenes fashion while both father and son pursued seemingly independent careers. In 1905 Dudley S. Liggett (1872–1933) established a real estate firm which obtained the contract to represent the Pennsylvania Railroad in purchasing and marketing its property west of Pittsburgh. At that time Dudley's father, Sidney B. Liggett (1849–1915), was secretary of the Pennsylvania lines west of Pittsburgh. It is astonishing that he was able to use an organization as large as the Pennsylvania Railroad to benefit a relative without himself occupying a top administrative position, though he did grant a benefit commensurate with the extent of his authority (west of Pittsburgh only). Also significant is that father and son have separate biographies in a biographical encyclopedia and neither biography mentions the other's occupation nor gives any hint of a connection between the two.[6] In this example the accumulation of advantages not only passed the benefit to the son as a result of the father's achievement, but also lent an aura of subtlety not given by outright employment in the family firm. Such cases create the illusion of greater career independence than actually existed.

Usually the son's dependence on the father is much easier to discern, as in the case of Jacob B. Negley (1833–1898). He became a banker in Muscatine, Iowa, but his bank suffered reverses when the depression of 1873 began. He returned to Pittsburgh the following year and immediately became the cashier of the City Deposit Bank. His father, George G. Negley (1808–1884), was founder and director of that bank. When the income provided by his bank position proved inadequate—he had married that same year—Jacob's father set him up in the insurance business.[7]

Sometimes the relationship between founding family members was more symbiotic than dependent, each person benefiting from the occupation of the other. John Phillips (1850–?) had been a farmer and dairyman but, in 1884, moved to McKeesport and set up a thriving grocery trade. His son Franklin (ca. 1875–?)took over the farm and supplied him with vegetables, dairy products, flour, meat, and honey. John obtained an advantage over his competitors by having a guaranteed supply of produce, while Franklin received the farm and a guaranteed market. This example can hardly be called a family firm but it is an instance of mutually beneficial interdependence.[8]

In other instances one may only infer a condition of dependence. John Liggett (1780–1833), for example, was first a cabinetmaker and then owner of a struggling tannery that was plagued by several fires. His fortunes suddenly changed after his marriage to Rosanna Sharp of a notable Philadelphia family which had founded Sharpsburg, Pennsylvania. He soon became associated with Leech & Co., transporters on the Pennsylvania Canal at Sharpsburg, where he occupied a responsible position.[9] While no recorded evidence indicates that he received help from his in-laws, his success after moving to a town founded by his wife's family, and perhaps still controlled by it, is certainly suggestive.

The previous examples show that in varying degrees and in varying forms the founding families rendered assistance to members who were not in a family firm. The individuals appearing in table 16 as having occupations outside the family firm may have been far less independent than the data suggest. While it is not possible to determine what percentage received assistance from the family, an estimate of 80 percent might not be excessive.

Ironically, some of the founding family members seemed to have believed that they were self-made men. The biography of Charles W. Anshutz (1840–1900), for instance, states that "he entered his father's foundry as a moulder, making his way step by step to his position as foreman of the works."[10] The biographer's usage of "making his way" suggests that his promotions were based on merit, not that they were a certainty due to his father's ownership of the business. Indeed, his biographer was far too modest, for Charles was not only foreman, he became a partner in the business.

Similarly, Thomas Rodd (born in 1849 of a Herron daughter) was educated at private schools and graduated from Annapolis before beginning as a rodman with the Pennsylvania Railroad in 1872. Within twenty years he was vice-president of the company. His biographer called his rise "meteoric," when it had been, to a certain extent, predetermined by his background.[11]

It is possible that the founding family members actually believed their success to be the result of their own efforts and accomplishments. The self-made man concept occupies a central position in American culture; the chance of getting to the top is, in America, a part of every man's birthright. Strangely, this concept may have been reinforced by the fact that the realization of their ambitions was not a certainty, even for the founding families. There were instances in every period of those who had accumulated so much and lost it.

Founding family businesses were ruined by any number of causes. It has already been noted how George Anshutz's iron manufactory was partly destroyed by the soldiers sent to suppress the Whiskey Rebellion. Thomas W. Bakewell (1778–1874) was a cotton buyer in New Orleans until he was ruined by the War of 1812. His first foundry, Prentice and Bakewell, had been established only two years when it failed in the depression of 1819. His second foundry, the firm of Bakewell and Cartwright, Founders and Machinists, was ruined by the 1837 depression. "He never regained his former financial footing." His brother, William Gifford, had backed his business with his signature and also went bankrupt. Thomas ended his career as a bookkeeper in Cincinnati and lived in retirement at his son's home in Allegheny City.[12]

Economic collapse was not the only source of trouble; natural causes also wreaked havoc. George Anshutz, Jr. (1781–1852), lost everything except for "what was on his back" in the Pittsburgh fire of 1845 as did William Eichbaum (1787–1866), a stockholder in Pittsburgh fire insurance companies and owner of a bakery and foundry, who "had been quite wealthy until he was ruined by the fire of 1845." Social upheaval was the undoing of Julian Neville (ca. 1807–1882), "a wealthy merchant of New Orleans before the Rebellion; an outspoken Union man, who was stripped of everything and died poor."[13] John C. Bidwell (1818–1891), husband of Sarah S. Dilworth, owned the Pittsburgh Plow Works which sold almost exclusively in the Latin American market; his volume of business was reduced sharply by the Cuban revolution of 1868–1878.

None of these reverses was due to business incompetence. True, Julian Neville caused his own undoing in that he did not act in his own best interest, but the others all fell victim to disasters beyond their control. This group provides a sharp contrast to those independently wealthy founding families who were insulated from the travails of seeking their own livelihood, since they never pursued an occupation.

Income derived from inherited wealth is commonly viewed as the patina on the upper-class family escutcheon. The privileged coupon-clipper is universally but quite inaccurately the stereotypical image of the upper class. Although most founding family members pursued intensive careers, a select few pursued no occupation at all save "curating" the family inheritance. Perhaps the successful investment of these assets was a full-time career. Harmer Denny Denny's (1852–1918) biographer makes no effort to conceal the fact that his entire business life was spent caring for his estate.[14] In 1888 his wealth was estimated at $500,000. The Dennys do approximate popular notions concerning the upper class. They repeatedly married other wealthy people—the O'Haras, and even other Dennys. Harmer Denny Denny was so named because his father, William Croghan Denny (1823–1866) married his first cousin, Elizabeth O'Hara Denny.

John Liggett (1821–1905) established a family tradition in spending his life in the "conservation and development" of his inherited estate, as did three of his five sons. One of them, William G. Liggett (1872–1923), found caring for money so attractive that he even retired from his law practice at age thirty-six to join his brothers "in taking charge of their father's estate."[15] Another son, John Liggett, Jr. (1859–?), pursued an independent career as a painter and musician, the organizer and sole support of the Pittsburgh Philharmonic Society. His patronage of the arts apparently was completely dependent on the family wealth.[16]

The founding family members who pursued business careers, however, were busily engaged and far from idle. Ironically, while they were the mainstay of founding family wealth, the aggregate record of success of those in business was below that of the professionals who presumably were dependent upon them.

The number of founding family members who were so rich that they could afford to spend their careers in philanthropy was always exceedingly small. The wealth necessary to support a career devoted solely to its care was equally rare in the founding families. The Dennys and the Liggetts are not archetypes; they are anomalies among the founding families whose wealth was historically based on a comparatively small start in an equally small community. It remained the task of succeeding generations to capitalize on the success of the family founder as that community grew. Despite the advantages passed on by their successful fathers, the majority of the descendants had to work for a living.

The accumulation of advantages, left unexploited, melts away. Popular literature is replete with stories of prodigals and profligates who squandered their fortunes in high living. These stories would not apply to many founding family members. Rare indeed was Presley Neville (1755–1818) who inherited a fortune but dissipated a great deal of it through extravagant living. He was forced to abandon the country squire life-style of his father and to sell all his possessions in an effort to escape poverty. In the manner of those family founders of humble origins, in 1816 he went to Ohio to claim the land previously granted to him in payment for military service. Most of the founding family members, however, did not waste their chances; they cultivated their opportunities with care through business enterprises or investment. In so doing they accumulated still greater advantages for their children.

The Professions

One common scenario for the acquisition of upper-class status is that the first generation accumulates wealth through business or trade, thus enabling succeeding generations to pursue the professions and the arts. Among the founding families, however, there was from the beginning a small group of professionals: doctors, lawyers, judges, engineers, scientists, authors, editors, architects, and professors.

Dr. Nathaniel Bedford (1760–1818), husband of Jane Ormsby, was reputed to be the first physician in Allegheny County. He and Dr. Felix Brunot, the only family founder in the professions, were among the incorporators of the Pittsburgh Academy. Harmer Denny (1794–1852), son of Pittsburgh's first mayor, was a five-term member of Congress and a law partner of Henry Baldwin, who was later appointed to the U.S. Supreme Court. Denny married Elizabeth O'Hara, heiress to the O'Hara fortune, thus becoming the richest founding family member. Other early prominent lawyers among the founding families were Morgan Neville (1783–1840), son of Gen. Presley Neville, and his cousin and law partner Neville B. Craig (1787–1863), son of Maj. Isaac Craig and Amelia Neville. Their legal associate was Walter Forward, later secretary of the treasury under President Tyler. All were men of power and distinction in their day.

John James Audubon (1780–1851), the French-born scientist and artist, became a member of the founding families when he married Lucy Bakewell. After a partnership with his brother-in-law, Thomas W. Bakewell (1778–1874), failed (they had opened a gristmill in Henderson, Kentucky), Audubon painted and published *The Birds of America* (1838), gaining for himself international acclaim as one of the greatest ornithological scientists of all time.

The professions did become far more popular in succeeding generations but business remained the economic mainstay of founding family wealth. None of the preindustrial fortunes amassed by the family founders were so enormous that successive generations were freed from the need to work, if only at the careful management of their estate.

Jackson Turner Main described professionals in Revolutionary America as enjoying "large incomes, yet the esteem in which they were held was not always proportionate to their wealth."[17] For the founding family professionals, the opposite was true. While he enjoyed great prestige, Dr. Felix Brunot was unable to maintain his home on Brunot's Island in the Ohio River and was forced to sell. Morgan Neville fared even worse. His law practice, prominent as it was, could not generate enough income to pay the debts incurred by his father's extravagant life-style. "Once Lafayette came to visit Neville in Cincinnati. He [Lafayette] asked how he [Neville] was and he said, 'I spent everything I had to pay my father's debts.' The general wrote a check on the U.S. Bank for $4,000 to Morgan Neville who was too proud to use it. His family, however, inherited it and also received a pension from Louis Philippe."[18] Neville's circumstances are an extreme example. Not all experienced financial difficulties; indeed, most probably lived quite comfortably.

The number of founding family members attracted to the professions, and the proportion that this number represents, increased markedly in each succeeding time period. As shown in table 17, more than one out of every ten founding family members was a professional in 1820, far above the national average, and by 1900 the ratio had risen to nearly one out of four. There are a number of reasons to explain this extraordinary occupational shift. Certainly the older, more traditional ways of earning a living were still available. Although some, such as commission merchant or landholder, were less certain as a means of advancement, opportunities continued in manufacturing and other commercial pursuits. Nonetheless, the founding families were drawn to the professions. Part of this change is represented by a shift inside the professions. The numbers given in table 17 do not include the clergy or military, groups that will be given separate consideration. These were occupations that lost popularity in the second half of the nineteenth century. Often the sons of military officers or clergymen, while not following their fathers' careers, did enter one of the professions. Rev. William Miller Paxton (1824–1904), who married Harmer Denny's daughter, was a professor at Western Theological Seminary in Pittsburgh and went on to become the president of Princeton Theological Seminary. His son, James

TABLE 17
Founding Family Professionals, 1820–1900

	1820 (N=111)		1860 (N=244)		1900 (N=263)	
Professions	12%	(13)	15%	(37)	23%	(61)
All other occupations	88	(98)	85	(207)	77	(202)

D. Paxton (1872–1944), a Princeton graduate, became a civil engineer. Likewise John Sturgeon (1865–1917), whose father Hugh Sturgeon (1822–1903) was a minister, became a lawyer and set up a practice in New Orleans.

Training for the professions was becoming increasingly formalized. Apprenticeship to a lawyer or a physician was supplanted by professional education at a university. One reason why the professions grew so dramatically among founding family members was the families' ability to finance the expensive education that was gradually becoming a prerequisite for entrance. Accompanying the higher, more standardized requirements for admittance into the professions was an increase in the rewards, as measured in income and prestige. The professions generally were becoming more lucrative, not only in medicine, but especially in law where the family name and connections helped to secure notable clients.

While business was still more financially rewarding, the professions were undoubtedly "safer." Repeated depressions occurring in the business cycle brought many founding family businesses to ruin, but the professions tended to be protected from this instability. Moreover, the professions were relatively free from the rapidly changing technologies and sharp competition characteristic of business. And lastly, there were finite limits to the number of relatives that even the healthiest of family firms could support. It was therefore necessary for some of the family members to seek independent careers.

Although the percentage of core and non-core founding family members in the professions is about the same, a slightly larger number of non-core members were professionals. Core members may have been more tied to the family firms and less able to pursue independent professional careers. Or core members may have felt a greater pressure to engage in more remunerative pursuits. Possibly founding family daughters selected mates from among professionals who were suitable partners in terms of prestige if not wealth. The professions probably offered non-core individuals an opportunity to marry well.

Certain founding families had a professional orientation,

others did not. In the Brunot family, where the percentage was highest, 71 percent were professionals. This does not necessarily mean a tradition in a single profession; two of Dr. Brunot's six sons were physicians and two were lawyers. In terms of professional continuity, the Sturgeon family must surely rank among the top with their involvement in medicine. When Dr. Daniel Sturgeon (1789–1878) established a practice in Uniontown, Pennsylvania, in 1813, he also established a tradition; his son, grandson, and great-grandson continued his practice in that town for well over a century.

The professional orientation of some of the families was not based on a love of the profession for its own sake. The professions afforded a high rate of success. Only three founding family professionals were marginally successful and none were unsuccessful. Despite this remarkable success rate, a significant number, twenty-three in all, chose to leave their professions in favor of another occupation. Seventeen percent abandoned the professions. They did so at a consistent rate for all time periods. The rate of abandonment by the core was more than twice that of the non-core, because more attractive circumstances awaited them upon leaving. Both groups were highly successful in their new careers. Those who continued in the professions sometimes abandoned their practice for a period of time, switched to another profession, or concurrently pursued outside interests as a means of self-advancement.

William F. Bakewell (1823–1900) was a lawyer, but from 1842 to 1900 he was also secretary of the Monongahela Navigation Company. William B. Negley (1828–1895) was at once a lawyer in the firm of Mellon and Negley and director of Citizens National Bank. Some left their professions for another profession. Morgan Neville abandoned his law practice to become the editor of the *Cincinnati Commercial Register;* Alexander Gilfillan (1857–1934) left civil engineering—he had earned a degree from Western University (University of Pittsburgh) in 1879—to become a lawyer. Still others left public practice but continued to use their professional expertise. Dr. Daniel Sturgeon (1789–1878), for example, was for many years the coroner of Fayette County, Pennsylvania. And numerous founding family lawyers became judges or were elected to public office, never to practice again. Others did leave the professions entirely but returned. Dr. Daniel Sturgeon's son, Dr. William H. Sturgeon (1826–1900), who inherited the practice in Uniontown, Pennsylvania, left to become director of the U.S. Mint and returned to medicine eight years later. A small proportion of those leaving the professions was accounted for by job promotions. In the early 1850s, Joseph N. DuBarry (1830–1892), husband of Caroline Denny, was engineer in charge of construction on the Pennsylvania Railroad. After at least nine promotions over a period of thirty-eight years he became second vice-president of the line, no longer an engineer. Finally, an even smaller number left their nonprofessional occupations in favor of a professional career. Such was the case of George W. Fahnestock (1823–1868), whose inheritance of $500,000 from his father enabled him to escape the tedium of mercantile life which was "uncongenial to his tastes." He became a naturalist, subsequently affiliating himself with the Academy of Natural Science, the Pennsylvania Horticultural Society, and Lafayette College in Easton, Pennsylvania.

If founding family daughters tended to select husbands from among the professionals because of the prestige the professions carried, they certainly made some outstanding choices. Among the non-core family members were professionals of national fame and prominence. John James Audubon, mentioned above, was the husband of Lucy Bakewell. Dr. William C. Gorgas (1854–1920) married Maria C. Doughty, a Guthrie. He is credited with the elimination of yellow fever and malaria while serving as chief sanitary engineer of the Panama Canal Commission in 1904. Sarah Ormsby married Charles Gustavus Roebling (1849–?), the engineer who carried on the work of completing the Brooklyn Bridge when death stayed the hand of his even more famous father, John Augustus Roebling. A Philadelphian, Edgar Viguers Seeler (1867–1929), husband of Martha Page Laughlin, also had a career in architecture. After graduating from the Massachusetts Institute of Technology in 1890, he studied in Paris in the Ecole des Beaux Arts for three years and then several more months in Greece and Constantinople. As an architect he taught design at the University of Pennsylvania for five years before turning all his energies to his own practice. A director of the Institute of Architects and a member of the Society of Beaux Arts Architects, Seeler was appointed a trustee of the Pennsylvania Museum and the School of Industrial Art.

Not all greatness was realized by judicious marriages of founding family daughters. The lineal descendants of the family founders were not without professional greatness of their own. The son of Eliza Herron, George Shiras, Jr. (1832–1924), was appointed to the U.S. Supreme Court in 1892. Dr. Daniel Sturgeon was twice elected U.S. senator from Pennsylvania, serving from 1840 to 1851.

The innovations made by the founding families in business had, from the start, a counterpart in the professions. Dr. Felix Brunot was the first physician in the country to use electricity in the treatment of disease. In the manner of Benjamin Franklin, Dr. William M. Herron (1823–1889) in the 1850s erected an observatory equipped with four telescopes. Acknowledged as an astronomer by John A. Brashear, he was a driving force for the construction of Allegheny Observatory. Similarly, Dr. Benjamin A. Fahnestock (1799–1862), a physician who accumulated a huge fortune in the wholesale drug business, was also a botanist and horticulturalist. He is also noted for introducing improved strains of poultry and livestock.

By the late nineteenth century some of the more prominent and innovative founding family professionals began to perceive the need for a systematized approach in order to effect desired change. The career of Thomas Liggett (1857–1942) was typical of the new professional during the Progressive Era. He was as much influenced by his inheritance of his father's vast real estate holdings as he was by his experience as an attorney. Concerned from an early date with the need for conservation, especially of lumber resources, he tried to interest the Pittsburgh Real Estate Board and the Chamber of Commerce in the rational use of the state's lumber reserves. But these locally oriented organizations were interested in development, not conservation. Finding their outlook too parochial, he joined the Pennsylvania Forestry Association and the National Conference on State Parks. The latter organization attempted to keep certain lands from "development" by having them set aside. Further pursuing his interests in conservation, Liggett joined the Valley Forge Association and the Save the Redwoods League, but his greatest achievement was the organization of the Cook Forest Association, a project "near and dear to his heart."[19] Through considerable effort, he, as secretary of the organization, persuaded the state to allocate $450,000 toward the purchase of the last remaining stand of virgin forest in Pennsylvania. The funds were insufficient, however, so he and the Mellon family raised $200,000 from contributions and from their own pockets.

In many of his conservation efforts, Thomas Liggett realized the need for public support. In 1911 he helped to organize the Boy Scouts in Allegheny County. He perceived the organization as an educational vehicle through which the public could be reached.[20]

Thomas Liggett represented the new professional with a broader, multifaceted outlook, but he was the product of a long line of development and heir to a tradition of social advantage which spawned it.

The Clergy and Military

The clergy and the military occupy a distinct position in American society. Both are perceived as motivated by high ideals, such as commitment to God or country, and disdainful of more mundane concerns. This distinction is emphasized by both garb and life-style. The collar and robes of the cleric and uniform of the military officer separate them from other occupations. They are not merely the gear of a particular occupation to be removed at the end of the working day; they constantly stand as a reminder of a particular calling. Likewise, place of residence is not an individual choice; both groups live in proximity to their fields of activity, in parsonage or officers' quarters. In addition, society sets a higher standard of behavior for its clergy and military. A vocation to either has usually been regarded as a lifetime career.

In American society, the social status accorded the clergy was traditionally high, but it declined somewhat during the nineteenth century.[21] Interestingly, the decline in the number of founding family members who chose the ministry as a career paralleled the declining prestige of the clergy.[22] Table 10 above shows a 0.7 percentage point decrease in the clergy based on a total of twenty-five individuals. Actually thirty-three founding family members were practicing ministers at one time but eight left their congregations.

Fully three-fourths of all the founding family clergymen were born prior to 1840. Clergy among the core group were concentrated in the earlier time periods: not a single core group member who was born after 1860 chose this profession. Slightly more of the non-core group entered the ministry and persisted in doing so throughout the nineteenth century. As was the case with non-core professionals, these individuals were considered suitable marriage partners for founding family daughters.

The decline in the number of founding family ministers after 1860 was accentuated by the fact that seven of the ministers resigned their pastorates. Rev. Scott Ingalls Wallace (1871–1953), husband of Mary Herron, left to start a kindergarten in Los Angeles; Caroline Denny's husband, William Paxton (1824–1904) became a professor at Western Theological Seminary; and Rev. Aaron Williams (1807–1878), who married Jane Herron, the daughter of Rev. Francis Herron, was appointed principal of Edgeworth Female Seminary. Not all left willingly: Rev. John Sturgeon (1827–1910) held a license from the Monongahela Presbytery since 1849, but it was withdrawn in 1864. The family history gives no explanation.

While not all seven may have removed the collar, they did cease ministering to a congregation, either to improve their lot, or simply because they tired of the ministry. At least five ministers changed their denominational affiliation, typically to a more respectable church. Three abandoned an "enthusiastic" Presbyterian sect in favor of a more staid form of Presbyterianism. The greatest number of denominational changes was made by Rev. William J. Bakewell (1794–1861). At first an Episcopal minister, he became a Unitarian, then returned once again to the Episcopal fold before becoming a Roman Catholic. He returned to the Episcopal ministry yet a third time, finally resigning his rectorship to become a teacher. No other minister changed denominations more than once.

Bakewell's career illustrates another point regarding change of religions. While he was a Unitarian, he opened a Unitarian school in Pittsburgh that was subsidized by his cousin, Benjamin Bakewell. When his Unitarian benefactor died in 1844, the school abruptly closed and Rev. Bakewell soon returned to the Episcopal church. He was not alone in making the necessary religious change when the situation demanded it. After a number of menial assignments including such places as Sugar Creek, Pennsylvania, Rev. Allan Campbell (ca. 1795–?), son-in-law to Benjamin Bakewell, left the Associate Reformed church and, in 1820, joined the Presbyterian church where he was promptly made pastor of a congregation in Nashville of which Andrew Jackson was a member.

A minister need not change denominations, however, in order to improve his social or economic condition. If a founding family minister did not receive a suitable congregation, he often moved to another. On the average, founding family ministers held 4.7 assignments. Only two held the same pastorates for the entirety of their careers; at least four held six different assignments. The frequency of change, about average for nineteenth-century clergymen, was fairly uniform throughout the century. Not suprisingly, each new pastorate was normally more desirable than the previous one.[23] Equally unsurprising is the fact that founding family ministers tended to hold wealthy urban pastorates. For example, Rev. George A. Lyon (1806–1871), husband of Mary A. Herron, was made pastor of a Presbyterian church in Erie, Pennsylvania, recognized as "one of the most prominent in the city."

While it is true that the founding family clergy did rather well for themselves, some evidence exists to show that they received assistance from other members of the family as those in business did. In addition to subsidizing his cousin's Unitarian school, Benjamin Bakewell in 1828 built Maple Grove, an estate overlooking the Ohio River, for his daughter and her husband, Rev. Allan Campbell. The fathers of Rev. Sanson Brunot (1808–1833), and Rev. Levi Risher (1836–1894), son of Nancy Denny McClure, donated land and built churches for them. Assistance was given in nonmonetary ways as well. Rev. William Paxton was appointed a professor of Western Theological Seminary while his mother-in-law, Elizabeth Denny, was associated with that institution. Perhaps more than moral support is implied in his biographer's account of his wife: "It is said that Caroline Sophia Denny contributed much to her husband's success." The aid given by Elizabeth Denny may have been his main chance: Paxton later became president of Princeton Theological Seminary.

After 1860, there were no more donated churches or free houses. It is a matter of conjecture whether the decline in the number of founding family clergymen resulted from a decline in family support or simply from lack of interest in ministerial careers.

Whereas all the clergymen were found to be successful, the same was not true of the military. Their rate of success was actually below that of the founding families generally, 71 percent for the military as compared to 75 percent for the whole. None of those in the military were unsuccessful, however. Many had no long-range commitment or love of military life; they served as officers or enlisted men during periods of war and then abruptly abandoned the military when peace came. Almost all wartime duty was performed from an officer's position and viewed as an opportunity to share in the excitement, test one's mettle, and collect honors. With this peculiar occupational perspective in mind, military men were divided into three groups for this study: those whose entire careers were spent in the military; those who were career men but left, actively pursuing other occupations; and those whose only work record was in the military but apparently did not pursue military careers. The work record of this last group occurred during a period when the United States was at war and their stay in the military was probably only for the duration. This group of eight men includes some who died while in the service, and will be eliminated from the statistical calculations.

Table 18 shows the distribution by year of birth of those who stayed and those who left the military after a period of service. It also shows the percentage of the military men from both groups who were marginally successful in each period.

Twenty-eight men (65 percent) spent their entire careers in the military, and fifteen left to establish other careers. Although highly concentrated in the first period, both groups experienced a sharp decline in number over time, probably in proportion to the decline in social status experienced by the military during relative peace.[24] Of those born after 1860, only three made a career of the military, for the advantages attendant to it were slim indeed compared to what they had been in the founding period.

Four of the family founders served for a considerable time in the military: Denny, Guthrie, Neville, and Phillips. Three of them profited materially from it; for Ebenezer Denny, it was his main chance. In later periods, however, the number who experienced only a marginally successful career continued to increase to a rate greatly exceeding that of the founding families as a whole.[25] All but two of the marginally successful had no careers other than the military. Thirty-six percent

TABLE 18
Military Service and Rate of Success by Date of Birth (N=43)

Years of Birth	Stayed in Military		Left Military		Total		Percent Marginally Successful
Before 1819	54%	(15)	47%	(7)	51%	(22)	18%
1820–1839	14	(4)	33	(5)	21	(9)	33
1840–1859	25	(7)	13	(2)	21	(9)	33
After 1859	7	(2)	7	(1)	7	(3)	67

of these career men were marginally successful compared to only 13 percent of those who left the military.

It may well be that those who left did so to pursue more attractive opportunities that did not exist for the career men.[26] In some instances their biographers make no effort to conceal this fact. Capt. Thomas J. Brereton (1822–1870), for example, resigned "to manage the large estates of Mrs. Denny," his mother-in-law. But others, such as Lt. Elias Phillips (1799–1856), "resigned, tiring of the inactivity of army life."[27] After more than ten years as a lieutenant, it is possible that he also tired of the infrequency of his promotions. Another who had a comfortable position awaiting him was Maj. James Verner Guthrie (1840–?), who became vice-president of the Lafayette Bank of Cincinnati. Without question, the most notable founding family member to leave the military for a better opportunity was the husband of Julia Dent (a Wrenshall daughter), President Ulysses S. Grant (1822–1885). ·

It is impossible to determine if those who remained in the military did so because of a lack of outside opportunity, because of their own doubts of the possibility of success in civilian life, or because they were truly committed to their chosen career. True, the success rate was 22 percent higher among those who left, but perhaps those staying were more committed to the military and therefore conceived of themselves as successful on their own terms. For one thing, those who stayed were far more likely to be a service academy graduate (29 percent) as compared to those who left (7 percent).[28] It is entirely possible that a service academy education alone would have produced a measurable increase in commitment to that branch of the service. In addition, a difference can be found between the core and non-core, the latter being considerably more likely to remain in the military.[29]

Like the "Philadelphia gentlemen," the founding families valued military service, but this was especially true during wartime. The Civil War offered an excellent opportunity to earn military laurels, particularly if a "suitable" position could be found. In the early months of the war considerable shuffling occurred on the part of the founding families to obtain the best possible positions.

In April 1861, only days after the bombardment of Fort Sumter, Albert Fahnestock (1834–1924) enlisted and became second lieutenant of a company not from Allegheny County. Three months later he resigned and quickly reenlisted as a first lieutenant with another company, this time one recruited in Allegheny County. Apparently, if a founding family member were not accorded an acceptable position elsewhere, he was able to return to Allegheny County and utilize the family influence to receive the treatment he "deserved."

Much the same was true of Oliver Shiras (1833–1916), son of Eliza Herron, who was assigned to the infantry. He was soon reassigned, made a first lieutenant, and placed as an aide on the staff of his second cousin, Gen. Francis Jay Herron (1837–1902). Shiras was able to repay the debt to the Herrons later when he, as U.S. judge of Iowa's Northern District, appointed one of the younger Herrons clerk of courts. Still more fortunate was William B. Negley (1828–1895) who was appointed a major and chief of staff for a major general who happened to be James Scott Negley (1826–1901), his first cousin.

If friends or relatives with influence couldn't be found, it was possible to "purchase" a position. Felix Casper Negley (1825–1901), after contributing $50,000 to the Union cause, was promptly appointed a major in the army. If neither of these avenues was open or desirable, a founding family member could organize his own military unit. Francis A. Dilworth (1840–1888) recruited a company at his home on Coal Hill (Mt. Washington), took it to Harrisburg in 1862, and was commissioned a lieutenant. That didn't satisfy him, however, and he was quickly promoted to captain of the company. Alexander Nimick (1820–1898) had less trouble having himself appointed captain of the Pittsburgh Rifles, which he also organized, since he equipped them at his own expense.

In addition to a suitable position in the military, it was necessary to enlist with the "right" military unit, for units were stratified in much the same manner as the city's social organizations. One of the most prestigious was the Pittsburgh Blues. "They were the first military organization in the county of Allegheny; were composed of the best material, and made up of members of the best families in the city and county."[30]

William G. Johnston (1828–1913), a volunteer in the Mexican War, made a poor choice in selecting a suitable military unit. He writes of his enlistment as a young man: "The day following, I made known to my father what I had done. He was greatly displeased, particularly on account of the company I had chosen. After some severe reflections, he wound up by saying that if I was intent upon going, I should not have enrolled myself with such men, but with those having some pretense of respectability. He was undoubtedly right." Evidently the military agreed with William's father, since the unit with which he enlisted was never called up for service and William missed the war.[31]

The accumulation of advantages functioned even in battle. At least three founding family members were captured by the Confederates, and all three were promptly released in prisoner exchanges. Felix Brunot served only eight days in the infamous Libby Prison before his release. Presley Neville Guthrie (1840–1948) and Francis Jay Herron (1837–1902) experienced similar brief incarcerations.

After ending their military careers, only four founding family members joined a veterans' organization. Among the family founders, only Ebenezer Denny is known to have belonged to the aristocratic Society of the Cincinnati. This organization of officers who had served in the Revolutionary War was never popular in the West, and it is interesting that Maj. Denny, whose social origins were below that of the other military family founders, should have chosen to belong.[32] Two others belonged to the GAR. Allan C. Bakewell (1847–1919) became department commander of New York, and Lewis A. Anshutz (1863–1937) advanced to lieutenant colonel in the Pennsylvania State Militia after thirty-eight years of part-time service. His military service was concurrent with his work in the family firm. Anshutz belonged to the Military Order of Foreign Wars, Spanish War Veterans, and American Legion.

Among the founding families, the role of the clergy and the military were similar in several respects. These vocations seemed to have undergone parallel changes in social status, and the founding families' response was a gradual decline in the number choosing these careers. Unlike the other professions, both the clergy and the military suffered a high drop-out rate which accelerated the decline in the percentage of founding family members in those occupations.

While founding family vocations in the clergy and military may have decreased due to a decline in social status those positions afforded, those who left were rewarded with substantial financial success in their new occupations. As Baltzell observes, "In the course of the nineteenth century, the ancient ideal of the chivalrous gentleman soldier, duty-bound and driven by the quest for glory, was gradually replaced by the more acquisitive ideals of bank and *bourse*."[33]

Government

If Ulysses S. Grant, husband of Julia Dent of the Wrenshalls, was the founding family member to achieve greatest renown in government, he was not the only one to become actively involved in governmental service. Besides a president of the United States, the founding families also produced George Shiras, Jr. (1832–1924), of the Herron family, who served as a Supreme Court justice; Daniel Sturgeon (1789–1878), who was elected for two terms as senator from Pennsylvania; and George W. Guthrie (1848–1917), who won the position of mayor of Pittsburgh by the largest vote ever polled and was later appointed ambassador to Japan. Although not as prominent, other founding family members served as state legislators, judges, and in a wide variety of county and municipal offices.

In only seven cases among the 119 founding family members who served in government was the position the individual's first occupation. This was not surprising since election or appointment to major posts is dependent upon success in another capacity. Grant came from the military, having gained high visibility and respect as commander of the Union forces during the Civil War. Daniel Sturgeon was a noted physician in Uniontown, Pennsylvania, where he served as coroner of Fayette County before his election to the Pennsylvania state senate and later the U.S. Senate. Count Tullio Verdi (ca. 1840–?), husband of Rebecca Denny, was also a doctor, leading to his appointment in 1872 as commissioner of health in several cities in Europe. Most founding family members who participated in government came from the practice of law, and were, like George W. Guthrie and George Shiras, Jr., eminent lawyers in their own right.

The roads to political involvement were many. Charles M. Bakewell (1867–1957) had been a professor of philosophy at Yale before his election to the state senate and later to Congress as a representative from Connecticut. Thomas Liggett (1779–1854) had been apprenticed to a carpenter and worked as a contractor, eventually moving into real estate. He became county prothonotary in 1836 and was succeeded in the post by his son, Thomas Liggett, Jr. (1812–1851). Joseph Dilworth (1826–1885) was a businessman who founded an iron business, owned a wholesale grocery firm with his brother George, directed the Northern Pacific Railroad and the Citizens' National Bank, and was president of the National Iron and Steel Publishing Company before being elected to the office of Allegheny County commissioner where he strictly supervised the granting of saloon licenses. His zeal in office led to the trial and conviction of two fellow commissioners for corrupt practices. Founding family officeholders were frequently associated with "reform" factions regardless of the era in which they lived and regardless of the nature of the particular reform that happened to be in vogue during their careers. Pittsburgh's Mayor Guthrie (in office from 1906 to 1909), for instance, was the archetype of the Progressive Era mayor.

The list of founding family names in government included a president, a senator, 12 judges, 53 in federal or state offices, 32 executives in local offices, and another 20 in local offices in lesser capacities. Some offices, such as justice of the peace and coroner, did not require the abandonment of a private career. Where there was no obvious conflict of interest, some officeholders retained positions held previously, although they were not active in the enterprise. Most of those who did not retire from office or die during their terms returned to their earlier occupations. The majority held a single post, although several progressed from local to county to state offices in extended government careers.

A number of founding family members, as important and influential men of their day, were involved in government without a career change or an official post. Thomas W. Bakewell (1861–1909) was known to be a close friend of President Taft. George D. Edwards (1872–?), husband of Pauline Dilworth, helped codify the Pennsylvania state banking laws while continuing his career. Others served on many advisory boards at almost all levels of government.

Founding family members served in government in the "noblesse oblige" tradition of the wealthy. Several, like Felix R. Brunot (1820–1898), refused recompense for their services. Often government service was in an appointive as opposed to elected capacity. These men were energetic and progressive in governmental service, dedicated to reform. No record has been found of any personal disgrace or scandal involving any of the founding family members in office.

Conclusion

For most of the population, occupation more than any other single characteristic is the foremost indicator of social status. Members of the upper class, not dependent solely upon employment for their income, often find their social status less tied to occupation. In most cases they derive income from wealth that they did not obtain themselves. Baltzell states flatly that "all upper classes have been based on inherited wealth."[34] Consequently, they are not required to earn a living in the sense that the middle and lower classes are. It does not necessarily follow, however, that the upper class is a leisure class. In his scathing criticism of the upper class, Thorstein Veblen stated that because of its wealth, "any incentive to diligence tends to be of no effect," and that wealth requires the "abstention from productive work."[35]

Unlike the elite in late-nineteenth-century Pittsburgh, the founding families were not typically heir to huge commercial or industrial fortunes. Even those who managed an estate had to work to maintain and increase it. There were only five known founding family males who did not actively pursue an occupation. Even several whose health was poor found something to do. True, in the sole case where a day-to-day record was kept, that of Robert McKnight (1820–1885), whose wife was an heiress to the Harmer Denny fortune, it appears that the amount of work done was far from exhaustive, but the work record of the vast majority of founding family members indicates busy careers.[36]

In examining the work record, one pervasive theme through the professions and the clergy as well as business was the constant changing of occupations. Among those in business it might be expected, but doctors, lawyers, and ministers also left their professions when something more lucrative appeared. The search for the main chance or the break to an even better position was never ending. They opted to utilize the accumulation of advantages in every conceivable way. In doing this, they largely succeeded.

Perhaps those who were not successful, and there were many, provided a lesson for the successful. A reasonably remunerative occupation was not a luxury. Comparatively few founding family members were so wealthy that they could afford to sit back and rest. Nathaniel Burt noted that even among nationally prominent families with great wealth, the succeeding generations had to exert considerable personal effort in order to maintain the family's position. Those who sat and waited for the mantle of greatness to be placed on their shoulders merely because of their social position and wealth waited in vain.[37] If this were true of the Lees, Adamses, and Duponts, it was also true of such families as Anshutz, Negley, and Wrenshall.

VI

Geographic Mobility

Residence

AMONG ALL THE features of daily living which individuals hold important, the place of residence ranks high. This is especially true in urban societies, where population density results in a greater frequency of social interaction than is possible in a rural setting. In an urban context, place of residence often reflects socioeconomic status. In a society as culturally diverse as the United States, urbanites have historically divided themselves into neighborhoods along ethnic, social, and economic lines. One's residence and the neighborhood in which it is located are frequently indicators of one's level of success. The neighborhood in turn influences social contacts and the scope of opportunities they afford. Similar interests, club memberships, and church affiliations help form the social contacts through which marriage partners are selected and business associations are established. All of these help contribute to an equality of condition and a similarity of kind for neighborhood residents.

In a walking city, where all contacts can be made on foot, place of residence may be less important because both formal and informal relationships can be maintained with comparative ease. The city is essentially a single neighborhood. Thus, the concept of neighborhood may have developed more complex ramifications by the 1890s than it had in the early or even mid-nineteenth century. In other words, the importance which neighborhood was to play in much of the individual's basic decision making increased as the city's population and geographical area increased.

This is not to say that there was, even in the early period of Pittsburgh's history, a complete absence of residential differentiation. Some homes were always considered more desirable than others, as determined by geographical location and by the age and structural condition of the buildings. Map 1 shows the residence pattern in 1820 of Pittsburgh's upper class (everyone listed in Powelson's "Founding Families" who also appears in the *Pittsburgh Directory for 1819*[1]). It reveals a certain amount of residential selectivity even when Pittsburgh was a walking city. With only a few exceptions, the oldest and most densely populated area, bounded by Water, Fourth, and Weist streets and Chancery Lane, constructed in part of clapboard and some log buildings, was avoided by the upper-class elite. They also avoided the area of Second and Third streets between Ferry and Market, an ethnically mixed and partly Jewish area.

While those in the manual occupations were scattered residentially, perhaps due to age and income, those in the nonmanual occupations were more concentrated. Sixty-five percent of them lived in only one-seventh of the city's land area (all the land between the rivers up to Grant Street). Although this area (dotted line on map) had high population density—much of the city's land remained undeveloped—it appears that as early as 1820 there was agreement among the upper-class elite regarding the desirability of a relatively defined and compact area in which to live.

Map 2, also of Pittsburgh in 1820, shows the residential pattern of the founding family sample, both core and noncore. While the number shown is small, reducing its significance, much of the core group did live in the same area as Powelson's upper class, but the percentage of their concentrations there is substantially lower. Another portion of the core group, almost half, lived in the developing area above Smith-

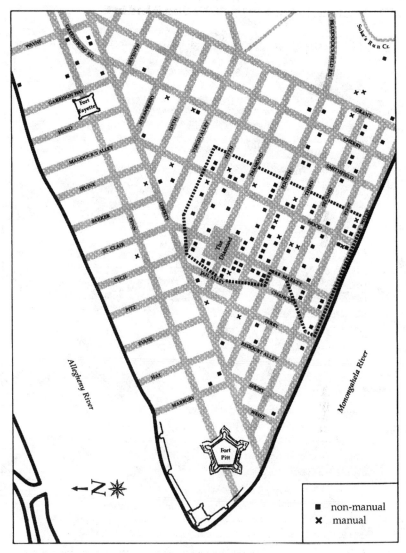

MAP 1. Residences of Powelson's Founding Families, 1820

Adapted from *Map of Pittsburgh and Its Environs,* surveyed and published by Jean Barbeau and Lewis Keyon, 1830, engraved by N. B. Molineaux, Pittsburgh.

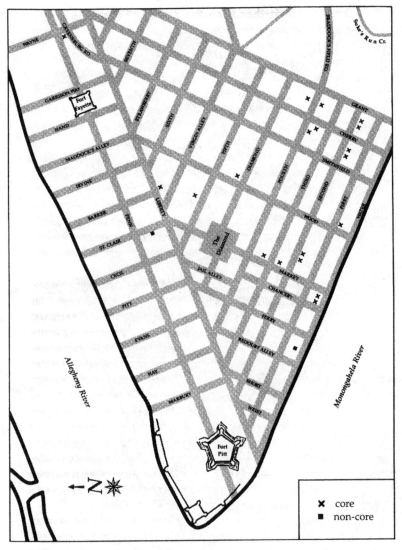

MAP 2. Residences of the Founding Families, 1820

field Street, still farther from the center of town. Generally though, neither the core nor the non-core group manifested any great degree of consensus in terms of residence in Pittsburgh in 1820.

In 1860, Pittsburgh still did not have an upper-class neighborhood in the modern sense. Both core and non-core families were scattered over a wide geographic area (map 3). Only three families lived in the old upper-class neighborhood. Those who remained in what was to become downtown lived on or near western Penn Avenue or near the foot of Grant Street, with an iron mill on the Monongahela River located only one block away. After 1860 the old city bounded by the rivers and Grant Street rapidly lost its appeal for the founding families. The total population of these four wards had continued to grow until 1850 as newer European arrivals settled there in affordable housing in close proximity to their jobs.[2]

As the center of old Pittsburgh lost favor, nearby Allegheny City, a separate municipality on the north side of the Allegheny River, experienced the greatest influx of founding family members. Their residences were not especially concentrated, though the non-core group had begun settling the so-called Mexican War Streets district, a pleasant area just north of the commons. Ridge Avenue, bounding the south side of the commons, was in the early stages of development as an elite neighborhood. In 1860 the South Side municipalities across the Monongahela River from Pittsburgh were at the peak of what little popularity they were to enjoy as an upper-class neighborhood. The only founding family members who did live there were the founders of the various municipalities (such as Ormsby) and their children after whom the streets were named (Sarah, Josephine, Jane, Sidney, etc.).

One obstacle to movement away from the central city was the lack of adequate transportation. Horse-drawn streetcars took two hours to make the run from East Liberty to the center of Pittsburgh. The isolation of East Liberty, still largely rural, was broken in the 1850s when the Pennsylvania Railroad opened a station there and another at nearby Shadyside. Oak-

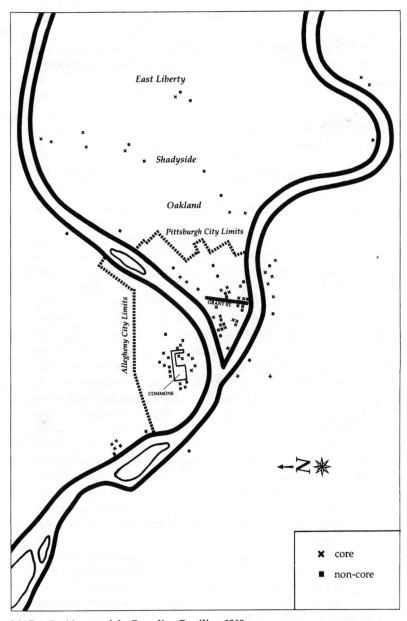

MAP 3. Residences of the Founding Families, 1860

land and East Liberty then became the main recipients of the outward migration. Seven nuclear families in East Liberty were descendants of the Negleys who owned the area originally. By 1900 the residence pattern had changed dramatically (map 4). Seven families (not shown) lived twelve miles west of the city in Sewickley (upwind of the smoke), an area on the Ohio River which developed quickly around 1900. (Some families moved there from Allegheny City.) Most notably, the city's East End had become the founding families' center of gravity. Only the Ridge Avenue area of Allegheny City, just past its peak as a desirable neighborhood, remained as a serious contender.[3]

This concentration in the East End paralleled the increasing degree of consensus within the founding families not only in terms of residential location and the high frequency of social contact which geographic propinquity afforded, but also in associated variables such as mate selection, religion, and general equality of condition. Indeed, it can be argued that geographic propinquity and equality of condition are so interdependent as to form a cycle in which one constantly reinforces the other. While it is difficult to identify the independent variable, a general equality of condition, especially economic and to a much lesser extent social, initially facilitated the movement of the founding families to the comparatively expensive homes in the East End. This ensured frequent social contact and intermarriage and, therefore, sameness of kind which, in turn, continued a general equality of condition. The formation of the East End as an upper-class neighborhood by 1900 was a necessary response to the increased size of the city if that identity and sameness of kind were to be maintained. Since the upper class had been able to maintain its identity in a smaller Pittsburgh of an earlier age, the formation of an upper-class neighborhood was not a coincidence. By 1900 Pittsburgh was the seventh largest city in the United States. This great urban center was becoming far more heterogeneous as successive waves of immigrants supplied the industrial demand for laborers. The enormous disparity in income and infusion of alien cultures caused the founding families to sort themselves out of the

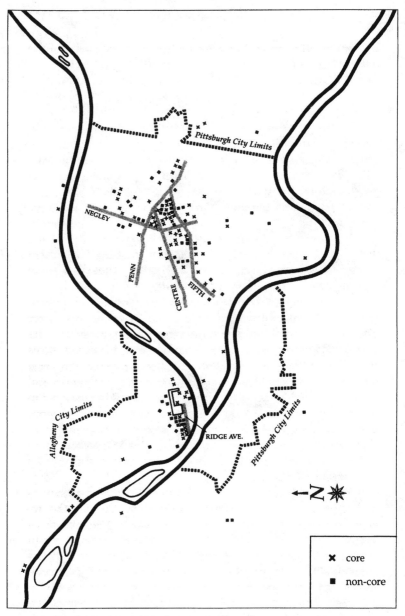

MAP 4. Residences of the Founding Families, 1900

general population and establish a homogeneous stronghold with those whom they recognized as their own kind.

Migration

During the nineteenth and twentieth centuries, industrial development in the United States was attended by a continuous redistribution of the population. This phenomenon profoundly affected the founding families whose success was predicated on the pursuit of new opportunities for advancement. In view of the family connections and other advantages already established in Allegheny County, it is surprising that any left at all since migrants have historically been those with the fewest community attachments. Yet there were a substantial number who did leave. Who were they? Where did they go? How did they fare?[4]

All social mobility studies which are focused on a given city or town must examine it over a period of time. Inevitably many of the people under observation move away and are thus "lost" from the statistical compilations. Nearly all these studies speculate that those who left experienced the same rates of upward or downward mobility as those remaining. Therefore these studies have meaning and relevance only in the place surveyed and only for that part of the sample population that never left. It cannot be assumed, however, that individuals migrating from the area experienced the same rates of upward or downward socioeconomic mobility as those remaining.

Following the outmigrants and assessing their success is an arduous and often disappointing task. Despite the researcher's best efforts, many individuals simply cannot be traced. Nevertheless, this study attempts to examine a given place and to relate it to geographic mobility in order to determine the relative proportions of outmigrants and nonmigrants, their changes over time, and the association between migration and vertical mobility. The main objective is to determine how successful in terms of occupation the migrants were in relation to the nonmigrants. The three success categories defined in chapter 5 (successful, marginally successful, and unsuccessful) are used again here.

To insure that only meaningful (that is, career-based) migration is taken into account, the following were excluded: the family founders, child migrants, college students, those who died in war, those whose entire careers were spent in the military, those who died before establishing a full work career, single women, and those who migrated after retirement. Movement within Allegheny County was not considered to be migration. In the remaining sample of 844 founding family members, 31 percent (265 individuals) were classified as migrants. However, of the initial group of 844, 57 migrants and 232 nonmigrrants were excluded because of insufficient career information, leaving a total sample of 555.

The figures shown in table 19 suggest that the rates of success for migrants and nonmigrants were much the same. This sustains the assertions of those researchers who discount the significance of outmigration in their studies. Indeed, the migrants are slightly more successful than the stay-at-homes. But the "migrant" category includes several different kinds of migration that had enormous impact on the founding families: migration out of Allegheny County; migration that excluded Allegheny County ("elsewhere-to-elsewhere" migration); and migration into Allegheny County. It is, then, only a table of migration per se.

A more accurate indication of comparative success would consider only outmigration from Allegheny County, that is, those individuals who left the local network of connections established by the founding families. It is this group who

TABLE 19
Occupational Success Rates for Migrants and Nonmigrants

	Successful		Marginal		Unsuccessful	
Migrants	76%	(158)	18%	(38)	6%	(12)
Nonmigrants	74	(257)	19	(65)	7	(25)

ventured forth, actively pursuing their own main chance in the tradition of the family founders. Such migration had brought great success to their fathers and grandfathers who settled in Allegheny County and might likewise profit them. But a 100 percent success rate was never realized by migrants, and starting over again in a new place presented formidable obstacles compared to the security of working in the family firm. Table 20 shows the success rates of outmigrants from Allegheny County over periods of time. The categories are arranged by date of birth; the date of migration is frequently unknown, but can be assumed as occurring at least eighteen years after birth. The sharp drop in the percentage of the successful from 76 percent for all migrants to 68 percent for outmigrants from Allegheny County indicates just how difficult it was to succeed outside the local network of family connections. This, however, should not obscure the fact that the majority of these outmigrants did succeed. In many instances they were still able to make use of the accumulation of advantages when it had a more national application. During the period of early development, when the founding families were still a heterogeneous local elite, migration from their narrow field of influence was risky. Migrants sometimes left without carefully considering their actions; they imagined opportunities that did not exist. Some farmers, for instance, moved time after time, eking out marginal livings and seeking

TABLE 20

Occupational Success Rates for Migrants from Allegheny County by Date of Birth (N = 94)

Date of Birth	Successful		Marginal		Unsuc- cessful	
Before 1820	50%	(15)	40%	(12)	10%	(3)
1820–1839	68	(15)	23	(5)	9	(2)
1840–1859	73	(19)	23	(6)	4	(1)
1860–1879	94	(15)	0	(0)	6	(1)
Total		(64)		(23)		(7)

better opportunities that they could not obtain. Four McClure brothers sold their farms in Allegheny County and moved separately to Ohio, Indiana, and Illinois. All four moved several times and were marginally successful, while their brother James McClure (1781–1861) stayed in the county, added to his farm, and was considered successful in business. Others followed more romantic dreams. John Howard Bakewell (1825–1849) was on his way to California to pan for gold when he died of cholera in Rio Grande City, Texas. Alexander Gorden Berthoud (1834–1893), son of Eliza Bakewell, went West only to spend the rest of his life working on steamboats.

With the passing of each successive time period, the number of migrants from Allegheny County decreased substantially, yet later migrants experienced a much higher rate of success. Moves tended to be more planned, often with a position waiting at the destinations. These later migrants, more likely to be professionals, moved within a national system with a far more elaborate infrastructure than had existed in earlier periods. They were able to use both family associations and corporate connections, as technology had permitted both to spread over a wide area.

When Thomas J. Brereton, Jr. (1858–1929), son of Amelia Denny, moved from Pittsburgh to Chambersburg in 1893, he did so to accept a position as a civil engineer for the Cumberland Valley Railroad. Thomas Bakewell Kerr (1849–1900), husband of Clara Dilworth, became a partner in the Bakewell law firm, enabling him to become general counsel for the newly founded Westinghouse Electric Company in Pittsburgh. When Westinghouse opened offices in New York City, Kerr moved there to form a new law firm. George Shiras, Jr. (1832–1924), son of Eliza Herron, was a prominent Pittsburgh attorney for thirty years. When he moved to Washington, D.C., in 1892 it was consequent to his appointment by Benjamin Harrison as a justice of the U.S. Supreme Court.

The professionals had never been as tied to place as the founding families as a whole. By the end of the nineteenth century, the professionals were joined by other occupational groups who were moving within large-scale systems, and not as a result of individual initiatives. Whereas early migrants had created their own situations, setting up practices and businesses, later migrants moved to accept positions in established institutions.

The clergy were a unique group in that they always resembled later migrants: they moved in order to assume positions waiting for them rather than to establish new churches. The risks they took in leaving Pittsburgh were therefore reduced and their success rates were extremely high. Indeed, their inclusion with other outmigrants tends to inflate the figures in the successful category for the early periods in which the clergy happened to be the most numerous. Without them, the remaining migrants in the earliest period actually experienced somewhat less than a 50 percent chance of success. Later, when there were fewer clergy to influence the statistics, the extremely high rates of success were due to the creation of organizational frameworks that offered other occupational groups the same kind of security that the clergy had always enjoyed.

Just over a third of the migrants are identified as "elsewhere-to-elsewhere," consisting of those who never lived in Allegheny County, since their parents or grandparents had previously left the county (table 21). At 84 percent, this group experienced an extremely high rate of success compared to only 68 percent for the group that migrated out of Allegheny County (table 20). This group was also predominantly non-core. These two facts correlate strongly, since many of the non-core elsewhere-to-elsewhere migrants were

TABLE 21
Occupational Success Rates for Elsewhere-to-Elsewhere Migrants (N = 73)

	Successful		Marginal		Unsuccessful	
Core	79%	(23)	21%	(6)	0%	(0)
Non-core	87	(38)	11	(5)	2	(1)
Total		(61)		(11)		(1)

successful professionals who married founding family daughters. Founding family daughters managed to choose husbands whose commitment to their profession was stronger than their attachment to place. These notables included not only the illustrious John James Audubon, Charles Gustavus Roebling, and William Crawford Gorgas, but also lesser lights such as Count Tullio Suzarra Verdi (ca. 1840–?), husband of Rebecca Adele Denny, who was appointed commissioner of health in several cities in Europe.

Among the other elsewhere-to-elsewhere non-core migrants were children of migrant parents who themselves continued to move in search of new opportunities, and short-distance migrants who were taking advantage of family business connections in other cities. John G. Muntz (1805–1880), husband of Mary B. Negley, owned a farm in Beaver County before moving sixteen miles to Zelienople, Pennsylvania, to join his brother in the operation of a store. This introduction to mercantile connections served him well in several other moves before he finally settled in Butler, Pennsylvania.

The elsewhere-to-elsewhere core migrants include children of Allegheny County parents who had migrated from the area. Their ties to the new place were not strong, and these children continued the pattern of migrration. General Presley Neville moved to Ohio to farm his land grant. His son Morgan abandoned a successful law practice in Pittsburgh to move to Cincinnati. Morgan's son Julian moved to New Orleans where he prospered as a merchant until the Civil War. In what is certainly a unique example, the Herron brothers, John (1857–1912) and David (1860–1920), were born in Dehra Dun, India, the children of missionaries. They returned to the United States, becoming civil engineers for western railroads. Both continued their careers as mining engineers in Montana, Idaho, Nevada, and Mexico before settling at the Tomboy Gold Mine at Telluride, Colorado.

Of the three kinds of migration that have been identified, by far the smallest was into Allegheny County from some other place, comprising only one out of every five migrants. This kind of migration was heavily concentrated in the earlier time periods. Of the forty-one individuals who migrated to Allegheny County after the family founders, thirty were born before 1840. This group was considerably more successful than the group leaving the county: 80 percent were successful, 10 percent marginally successful, and 10 percent unsuccessful. They were also fairly evenly divided between core (23) and non-core (18) both of whom perceived that opportunities or security awaited them in Allegheny County.

At least some of this migration can be identified as stem migration, since relatives followed the family founders. Family founder George Anshutz migrated to Allegheny County from Alsace in 1792. He was joined forty years later by his nephew Henry Anshutz (1812–1887) who had worked in Alsace as a patternmaker and was able to find employment with various foundries, although not directly in his uncle's iron works.

Some of the migrants to Allegheny County were children of founding family members who had left the area. They returned to pick up the family connections and accumulation of advantages that their parents had left behind. Ormsby Phillips (1829–1884) was born in St. Louis, but headed the telegraph office in Louisville before coming to Allegheny County and joining the firm of Anderson and Phillips, Iron Founders. He was elected mayor of the city of Allegheny, Pennsylvania, in 1875.

In like manner, Felix Reville Brunot (1820–1898), born in Newport, Kentucky, prospered in Pittsburgh despite his previous business failures in Rock Island and Camden, Illinois. In Rock Island he had entered the milling business and in Camden he was a wheat and grain dealer. Neither of these ventures had anything to do with his college training in civil engineering. His efforts in Illinois were to last only five years. Moving to Pittsburgh in 1847, Brunot became a partner in a steel firm and a trustee of two banks. By the 1880s he was a millionaire. Although his education had no more prepared him for banking than for business, the critical difference was location and not occupation. In Illinois the family name was unknown and family connections nonexistent. In Pittsburgh they meant everything. Only twenty years after moving to Pittsburgh, Brunot was so well established that, in the tradition of a gentleman civil servant, he served without pay as Indian commissioner under President Grant.

The advantages held by the founding families also benefitted many non-core people who chose to settle in Pittsburgh. Professionals particularly found their careers advanced upon marrying into the founding families. William McKennon Morgan (1823–1854) from Canonsburg, Washington County, studied medicine at the University of Pennsylvania, but set up a highly profitable practice in Pittsburgh where his wife, Jane Ormsby, although born in Louisville, retained family connections. Similarly, Hill Burgwin (1825–1898), born and educated in North Carolina, married Mary Phillips, daughter of Sarah Ormsby, and built a successful career as an attorney for several major banks and later as director of the Pittsburgh and Connellsville Railroad. William L. Pierce (1860–1919), a Dartmouth College graduate from Berkeley, California, married Flora McKnight, the daughter of Elizabeth O'Hara Denny, and set up his practice as a patent attorney in Pittsburgh. His move was undoubtedly influenced by his having studied law under another non-core member, George Shiras (1806–1892), the husband of Eliza Herron. Having been educated at prestigious institutions, these men probably would have prospered wherever they set up practice, but they chose to make use of family connections in Pittsburgh. The high degree of success they achieved indicates the wisdom of those choices.

Founding family members who migrated from Allegheny County did not necessarily burn their bridges. The accumulation of advantages could be seized again should they choose to return. Neville B. Dilworth (1848–1912) operated the Magnolia sugar plantation in Louisiana for his father until it was sold in 1871. At that time, having proved himself, he was made a partner in his father's wholesale grocery business, joining his two brothers in Pittsburgh. He left Pittsburgh four years later, however, to join the merchandising firm of Allen and Evans in New York City. From there he went to Montana to engage in contracting and then to North Carolina where he became a banker. Marrying Jessie Black, he returned to Pittsburgh in 1900. Dilworth was immediately taken on as a partner in Jessie's father's real estate company. This was fortunate for him, but having the name of Neville B. Dilworth attached to the S. W. Black Company was advantageous for the company as well.

The founding family members who chose to leave Allegheny County during the course of the nineteenth century clearly reflect the transportation possibilities available to them in the direction of their migration. Table 22 shows the general direction of their journeys.

One of the most striking aspects of the direction of migration from Allegheny County at different times is the heavy use made of the rivers in the earliest time period. Historically Pittsburgh was the embarkation point for western pioneers who had crossed the mountains and then sold their carts and wagons to travel downriver on the Ohio and Mississippi rivers. Although a regular service had existed between Pittsburgh and Cincinnati since about 1800, the building of the steamboat *New*

TABLE 22
Destination of Founding Family Members Leaving Allegheny County by Date of Birth

	-1819	1820–1839	1840–1859	1860–1879	Total
Western Pennsylvania	1	5	9	2	17
Ohio and Mississippi river valleys	16	1	2	3	22
Upper Midwest and West	12	15	15	8	50
South	3	6	9	4	22
East	2	3	8	3	16
Total	34	30	43	20	127

Note: Two founding family members migrated to foreign countries in 1820–1839 and 1860–1879. Numbers include individuals whose success category is unknown. Since the numbers have comparative value both horizontally and vertically, percentages are not given.

Orleans in Pittsburgh in 1811 catapulted Pittsburgh's commerce into a new era. It also confirmed the river as the dominant avenue used by western migrants. In the earliest period, of the thirty-four founding family members leaving Pittsburgh, sixteen joined this wave, settling as close as Youngstown and as far as New Orleans. Of all the river cities, Cincinnati claimed the greatest number of migrants, underscoring the strong relationship that city had with Pittsburgh. The founding family members who traveled downstream enjoyed a very high rate of success. Later, when railroads replaced water-borne transportation (and the Civil War altered travel patterns) there was very little movement downriver.

Some local migration to other areas in Western Pennsylvania occurred in each of the time periods. Generally these short-distance migrants were less successful than those who endured greater separation from home and family ties. Their ventures—buying a new farm, starting a grocery business, and so on—were often narrower in scope and more limiting in their potential rewards than the grandiose schemes envisioned by the long-range migrants.

It is sometimes difficult to assess the purpose behind migration, especially when a person moves not to accept an existing position, but to create a new one. Whether the endeavor was planned in advance or was the product of an "accidental" opportunity is difficult to distinguish. Undoubtedly those who knew precisely where they were going had the greatest chance of success. When Charles M. Bakewell (1867–1957) left his teaching position at the University of California in 1905, it was to accept a position as professor of philosophy at Yale University. And when James K. Doughty (1849–?), son of Martha Guthrie, moved to Kansas in the 1890s, he immediately became judge of Probate Court. His subsequent move to Colorado resulted in a similar success as he became the judge of Powers County. A principal factor which seems to characterize the successful is that they had obtained the position prior to leaving. Migration was part of a clearly defined objective.

Occasionally, however, it appears that when a founding

family member did not achieve to his satisfaction, he moved to a small town where he became part of the economic elite. Such seems the case with William H. Ritter (1843–?) who married Sarah Gibson, a Negley descendant. In Pittsburgh he was at various times a salesman and a clerk. By all indications he was not advancing, so with a partner he moved to Butler, Pennsylvania, and carried on the largest dry goods and millinery business in that town. Before succeeding in Butler, they had opened a store in at least one other town. In this instance, migration seems to have been part of a hit-or-miss proposition rather than an integral part of plans made in advance.

At times founding family migration may have been even more aimless, especially among the less successful. Henry P. Sturgeon (1827–1909) sold the farm left him by his father in 1856 in Oakdale, Pennsylvania, and moved to another farm in Ohio. In the space of fourteen years he owned or rented six different farms in eastern Ohio and Western Pennsylvania before finally moving to Beaver Falls, Pennsylvania. His movements, possibly associated with a lack of perseverance or even instability, brought him no appreciable success. Sturgeon's biographer notes the extent and frequency of his moves apologetically and attempts to save the rest of the family from the shame he supposedly brought on them: "His frequent changes of residence were due to a nomadic instinct that had developed in him alone, his forebearers ever having been content to remain in one place."[5] Obviously remaining in one place was considered a virtue associated with dependability.

In the previous discussion of residence, I noted that by 1900 the founding families had established to a greater degree than ever before a rather specific area of Pittsburgh as an upper-class neighborhood, and suggested that this may well have been an attempt to maintain the identity and homogeneity of the group in a growing city. It may have been more difficult for the migrants to adapt socially to a new locale than it was for the nonmigrants to differentiate themselves from the general population in Pittsburgh and Allegheny County. The nonmigrants had established relationships with each other based on something more than economic success. The migrants discovered that achieving economic success in new locations was quite different from finding social acceptance. By all appearances, however, most migrants who were successful were readily able to adapt to their new communities. They soon became prominent citizens, serving on boards of trustees and elected to local and state offices. After Charles M. Bakewell became a professor at Yale, he was elected to the state senate and later represented Connecticut in the U.S. House of Representatives. John Bennington Boggs (1809–1889), the son of Margaret Sarah Wrenshall, was born in Philadelphia but moved to Alabama. There he had little difficulty in finding social acceptance for he married Ann Houston, sister of the governor of Alabama. Other founding family members enjoyed similar social acceptance elsewhere.

Some, however, found the adjustment much harder. Julian Neville was very successful as a merchant in New Orleans, but his outspoken support of the Union during the Civil War led to financial ruin and social ostracism. William McClure (1810–1860) became quite wealthy in St. Louis, but his wife Margaret was such an ardent Southern sympathizer that she and her fourteen-year-old son were eventually arrested for assisting the Southern cause and banished to the South through the Union lines. Despite their material success, these people were not at home in their adopted societies. These cases, both of which occurred as a part of the social upheaval attendant to the Civil War, are exceptional. Julian Neville and Margaret McClure seemed to have fit into their respective social milieus until the war came. It was their self-proclaimed nonconformity in an atmosphere demanding total conformity that caused their rejection. In a very real sense, they caused their own alienation.

The social acceptance accorded to successful founding family migrants, especially in the later time periods, was due in part to the erosion of local and regional identities by 1900. Local upper classes were more open to penetration by outsiders because they shared similar values and life-styles. The new social and corporate networks drew these local societies to a recognition of their likeness of kind, a manifestation of the growing homogeneity of the American upper class. Like the proverbial chicken and egg, it becomes impossible to determine whether social acceptance led to financial success or vice versa, since the two were so interconnected and mutually supportive. Conversely, the marginally successful and unsuccessful migrants found themselves without the necessary connections to win them either social acceptance or financial success in their new location. Without social acceptance, it was impossible for them to gain access to credit facilities, market their goods or services or, for that matter, to enter any of the avenues of power and influence traditionally associated with success. Lack of financial success precluded the acquisition of any of the social distinctions that were necessary for acceptance into upper-class society. These founding family members had lost the accumulation of advantages. Unable to find either social acceptance or financial success, these migrants moved repeatedly in their vain attempts to realize either one.

Conclusion

Nearly a third of all founding family members moved away from their communities at some time during their careers. A change of such magnitude held profound consequences for the founding families. With time this migration was destined to spread these families across the United States and even to foreign lands. The reasons behind their moves were not too different from those motivating others who were moving from one place to another. Primarily they were seeking to "better" themselves. The positive desire to improve their condition was decidedly more important than the negative wish to flee an undesirable economic situation. In this they joined that larger stream of migrants headed westward. The more rural families gradually became a part of the rural-to-urban shift as the sharp drop in founding family members engaged in agriculture so graphically attests.

Through the course of the nineteenth century, a change occurred in founding family migration that underscored what was happening to the families within larger social and cultural contexts. Before the Civil War, both the direction and form of their migration resembled the larger national profile. As the traffic went to Louisville, Cincinnati, and St. Louis, so did the founding families, though their business interests often took them farther south than the larger stream of northern migration typically went. Founding family migration occurred within a framework of small interpersonal relationships that also characterized the larger population in preindustrial America.

After the Civil War, founding family migration changed radically, especially in its direction. Both the Civil War and the advent of the railroad had altered patterns of migration even as they had changed the larger society. However, as the larger stream of migration continued to head west, the founding families began moving in every direction. What inspired these moves was of greater importance than the move itself. Earlier in the century, migrants went to a city or, more frequently, a small town and started a business or a professional practice. By 1900 migration tended to occur within large-scale systems and was apt to be more economically stable. These later migrants moved to large urban centers where they assumed previously obtained positions. The evolution of these large-scale systems was facilitated by newly developed technologies. As a result, the nation was developing an upper class that was no longer merely a collection of locally or regionally based upper classes, but one that was increasingly national in character. The cement that would hold the national upper class together was marriage.

VII

The Family

Marriage

AN INDIVIDUAL'S closest and strongest social ties are normally within the family. Unlike other personal associations that one may develop through clubs, churches, social organizations, and neighborhoods, family relationships do not affect just a single aspect of one's life—they affect every aspect. Associations outside the family require less individual commitment; therefore the functioning of these institutions depends upon group consensus rather than upon individual control. Typically a single family cannot regulate the entrance of outsiders into such institutions, but they have considerable control over who marries into the family. In thus preserving its own social position and likeness of kind, the upper class has been generally regarded as more familistic than the rest of society, selecting marriage partners not only on the basis of their own merits, but also on their family's reputation.[1]

When a family has achieved high enough status for the individuals within it to be considered suitable marriage partners for sons and daughters of upper-class families, that family has become upper class. A single individual may attain vertical mobility through marriage, but when all the members of one family are considered suitable partners in upper-class marriages, it follows that the family is considered to be of near equal status. This equality of social class standing was evidenced by a number of cases among the founding families where brothers or sisters from one family married sisters or brothers of another upper-class family.

Historically the various social classes have not intermarried freely; a marriage is normally contracted between partners of roughly equal socioeconomic status.[2] Marriage gives to the couple jointly what had previously been individually assigned social standings. Therefore, it is an indicator of socioeconomic class standing in much the same way as are occupation, wealth, residence, or club memberships. In addition to this, marriage can be an indicator of still another phenomenon, the identification of suitable partners (people of similar standing) either inside or outside of each other's community. The development of a national upper class can be inferred by tracing the geographic distance over which marriages were contracted.

The marriages made by the founding families have been arranged into five categories with respect to the degree to which the marriage was endogamous—that is, within Pittsburgh's elite upper class. (It is the geographical origin of the marriage partners that is at issue, not the location of the wedding ceremony.) The first category, "Powelson's founding families," represents endogamy within the group named in Powelson's "Founding Families," including the twenty families in the sample.[3] The second category, Pittsburgh, includes all residents of the Pittsburgh area, though not necessarily natives, who are not listed in Powelson. "Out-of-town upper class" represents an increased degree of cosmopolitanization. It includes everyone born outside the Pittsburgh area, living outside the Pittsburgh area, or recently moved to the Pittsburgh area from elsewhere. Based upon available information (such as their occupations, or their father's) these people are believed to belong to a social and economic upper-class not rooted in the Pittsburgh area. The next category, Out-of-Town, represents the final and most extreme degree of cosmopolitanization. The residence requirements are the same as in the previous category, but the social requirements differ in that, based upon available information, the marriage partner is believed not to be a member of a social upper class or an economic elite.

A final category, "unknown," was created to include persons for whom information regarding place of birth or residence is lacking. Marriages to persons whose backgrounds are unknown have been included in the statistical calculations because this may be interpreted as a measure in itself. Precisely what is measured cannot be determined with certainty, but two speculations are possible: that they were not long-time residents of the Pittsburgh area and that they were probably not socially prominent.

Table 23 shows the marriages of the founding families by twenty-year periods (1780–1900). Marriages within the confines of Powelson's founding families accounted for 14 percent of the total, but that percentage varied greatly over the eighteenth and nineteenth centuries. In the first two periods, more than one out of every four marriages involved only this group, a rate that declined markedly to about 19 percent in the 1820 to 1839 period, and to 10 percent following the Civil War. Since the percentage of marriages made with Pittsburghers who were not listed in Powelson's "Founding Families" increased sharply after 1800, and since the county population increased an average of 5.3 percentage points per year from what it had been in 1800, it seems plausible that population increase was a factor in this decline. The post–Civil War figures may be attributed to a nationalization of the elite upper class were it not for the fact that the percentage of out-of-town upper-class marriages was so erratic. Indeed, this percentage declined after 1859 and never again assumed a significant proportion of the total number of marriages. The percentage for out-of-town marriages was similarly erratic.

Some proof supporting the theory that the upper class had become nationalized may be found if the statistics are combined. If the first two categories are combined to form a new category designated "local," and the remaining categories are designated "nonlocal," quite a different result is obtained (table 24). The nationalizing trend does not begin in the late

TABLE 23

Marriage Categories of the Founding Families

	1780–99 (N=26)	1800–19 (N=53)	1820–39 (N=98)	1840–59 (N=156)	1860–79 (N=220)	1880–[a] (N=234)	Total (N=787)
Powelson's Founding Families	27% (7)	28% (15)	19% (18)	17% (27)	10% (22)	11% (25)	14% (114)
Pittsburgh	15% (4)	21% (11)	16% (16)	15% (23)	20% (45)	10% (24)	16% (123)
Out-of-town upper-class	4% (1)	7% (4)	8% (8)	10% (15)	6% (13)	6% (15)	7% (56)
Out-of-town	15% (4)	6% (3)	8% (8)	11% (17)	10% (21)	12% (27)	10% (80)
Unknown	39% (10)	38% (20)	49% (48)	47% (74)	54% (119)	61% (143)	53% (414)

a. Includes some marriages after 1899.

TABLE 24

Local and Nonlocal Founding Family Marriages

	1780–99	1800–19	1820–39	1840–59	1860–79	1880–[a]	Total
Local	42%	49%	35%	32%	30%	21%	30%
	(11)	(26)	(34)	(50)	(67)	(49)	(237)
Nonlocal	58%	51%	65%	68%	70%	79%	70%
	(15)	(27)	(64)	(106)	(153)	(185)	(550)

a. Includes some marriages after 1899.

nineteenth century, but appears as early as 1820–1839 when nonlocal marriage partners outnumbered locals two to one. Baltzell found the nationalization of the Philadelphia upper class to be a post–Civil War phenomenon.[4] Among Allegheny County's founding families nonlocal marriages constituted almost two-thirds of the total in 1820–1839, an amount so large that later periods witnessed only minor increases. After 1880, an even greater percentage of marriages were nonlocal, however. It is reasonable to conclude that in the post-1880 period, when perhaps 79 percent of the marriages were nonlocal, the increase reflects the emergence of a nationalized elite upper class which in turn was the result of a centralized American economy. Even if an evolving national upper class is not confirmed by these statistics, the development of a national network of connections facilitating these marriages cannot be disputed.

The inclusion of unknowns who married into the founding families in the nonlocal data given in table 24 poses the question of whether these were marriages to a lower class. It is justifiable to question if the non-core were socially below and consequently dependent upon the core, especially in a financial way. Using Yule's Q to assess the degree of success of the core and non-core, it is possible to determine if a relationship existed between the core group and success and correspondingly, the non-core and the marginal or unsuccessful category.[5] Using this ratio, a result of +1 indicates a 100 percent correlation; −1 indicates a 100 percent negative correlation, meaning that the factors are inversely proportional; and 0 indicates no correlation. Thus, a Yule's Q of −0.06002 in this study reveals almost no relationship between the core and success. It also means that the categories other than "Powelson's founding families" or "out-of-town upper class" do not imply marriage to a lower class. It may also mean that the core was not necessarily "supporting" the non-core, or that if it were supporting the non-core, it supported it successfully. Otherwise a higher Yule's Q would result.

Since the father's occupation is of major importance in determining the socioeconomic status of the children, it is meaningful to compare the occupational distribution of the founding families with that of the fathers of all the non-core marriage partners (table 25). The average difference between the percentage of non-core fathers and founding families in a given occupational category was only 4.5 percentage points, indicating a close parallel between the two groups. Because the statistics for fathers are used for the non-core, the average distribution reflects an earlier occupational structure (one generation older) than for the founding families. As a result, the percentage of non-core fathers engaged in agriculture and the military more closely approximated that of the founding families in 1820 (26 percent and 11 percent respectively). Therefore, the already high percentage of non-core fathers in occupations with high social status becomes even more impressive. With the exception of banking and related fields, the background of the non-core resembled that of the founding families. Indeed, in the highly lucrative manufacturing field, the founding families' percentage never equaled that of the non-core families. The fact that the fathers of the non-core marriage partners were so

TABLE 25
Ooccupational Distribution of the Founding Families and Non-core
Fathers

Occupation	Founding Family (N=618)		Non-core Fathers (N=207)	
Professional	18%	(111)	18%	(36)
Clergyman	4	(25)	9	(18)
Banker/broker/insurance	15	(94)	5	(11)
Business executive	7	(44)	1	(3)
Manufacturing/construction	10	(64)	15	(30)
Mining/refining	2	(11)	1	(2)
Merchant	7	(42)	6	(13)
Keeper (store, etc.)	3	(19)	2	(5)
Government official	9	(56)	4	(9)
Clerk/laborer, etc.	6	(36)	1	(3)
Military	8	(48)	14	(28)
Agriculture	11	(68)	24	(49)

successful may initially tempt one to apply the observation of Charles and Mary Beard regarding the established families of Boston, New York, Philadelphia, and Baltimore: the old families with decreasing fortunes "escaped the humiliation of poverty by judicious selections from the onrushing plutocracy."[6]

Despite certain instances of core marriages to non-core money, the Beards' observation does not hold true for Allegheny County's founding family males. For example, a considerable portion of the Denny family wealth was accumulated through Harmer Denny's marriage into the O'Hara family. The marriage of Alexander Guthrie (1845–1899) to Mary Hussey enabled him to tap her father's wealth in order to become a crucible manufacturer. His brother George (1848–1917) married Florence Howe, yielding a similar bonanza; he became mayor of Pittsburgh and an ambassador to Japan. The Howe family wealth was also shared with another founding family. Florence Howe's sister Eleanor married Frank Bailey Nimick (1849–1924) who was involved in steelmaking, banking, and the operation of two of Pittsburgh's Mt. Washington inclines. The Herron brothers, Thomas G. (1851–1889) and John H. (1853–1933), realized great wealth upon marrying the daughters of Maj. A. M. Brown, a coal magnate. However, none of these marriages were to "onrushing plutocracy." The families were well established and of similar social status. Both the O'Haras and the Howes were listed among Powelson's founding families.

In terms of employment, less than 1 percent of all core males were dependent upon their fathers-in-law. Employment of males tended, in both core and noncore, to be with the father, not the father-in-law. Moreover, core group sons tended to select wives of equal or at least similar social background, whereas core group daughters married "new wealth" to a greater degree. The Beards' observation is therefore applicable to some founding family daughters who selected husbands from among the nouveaux riches.

When John Liggett married Rosanna Sharp of Sharpsburg (ca. 1810), he was able to use her family's wealth and connections to reestablish himself after repeated fires had ruined his tannery business. This, however, was not typical. Marriage into a prominent family more commonly indicates the success of that individual in making himself a suitable marriage partner. George Senft (1848–1885) married Keziah Jane Negley in 1884 after his first wife's death. His father was a German immigrant tavern owner who later turned to farming. Senft worked as a lithographer in Pittsburgh and New York before attending the Iron City Business College. With his newly acquired skills he became an assistant bookkeeper for the Mellon brothers' lumberyard in East Liberty. He worked his way up to cashier in the banking house of Thomas Mellon & Sons and eventually became superintendent and then general manager of the Ligonier Valley Railroad, for which he had increased ridership by creating Idlewild Park. It was only after he had attained his position with the railroad that Senft married a Negley daughter.

In a parallel story, Senft's employer, Thomas D. Mellon (1813–1908) had advanced his own position before marrying into the Negley family. Mellon's marriage to Sarah Jane Negley in 1843 was, by all accounts, the most notable founding family marriage of this sort. Sarah Negley's mother, Barbara Winebiddle, was a daughter of a prominent family of old East Liberty landowners who were listed in Powelson's founding families. At the age of five, Thomas Mellon had immigrated to Westmoreland County, Pennsylvania, with his parents to escape poverty in Northern Ireland. In 1832, Mellon moved to Allegheny County. Before his marriage to Sarah Negley, Thomas Mellon had managed to obtain a college education at Western University, gain admittance to the Allegheny County Bar, become a legal trustee of various large estates, become an "operator of coal mines," and owner of extensive real estate. It was an auspicious beginning, but before he was finished, the judge (he was elected judge of the Court of Common Pleas in 1859) established the banking house of Thomas Mellon & Sons in 1870 and purchased the Ligonier Valley Railroad in 1877. His banking house became the foundation for the greatest founding family fortune. It was this non-core family that went on to become the most powerful in the city—nationally known yet identified with Pittsburgh.

More frequently, however, founding family daughters married second-generation, not first-generation, wealth. This should not be taken as an instance of "marrying down," since in the 1820 period many founding family daughters were, themselves, second- or third-generation wealth.

Economically, marriage between core and non-core could involve far more than the simple financial dependence of either partner. In the process of transforming an economic elite into an upper class, marriage was frequently a vehicle for consolidating and perpetuating economic power. Even though these marriages were not formed solely for mercenary reasons, they did occur as a natural consequence of the social, technological, and economic realities of the time. Families with similar interests and ambitions pooled their resources and management capabilities into closely knit networks.

Figure 6 illustrates how some of the founding families were united by bonds of business association as well as matrimony. The diagram shows two families, Johnston and Anshutz, who were not intermarried and had no direct business ties. Yet the marriage of Rebecca Johnston to William Eichbaum in 1814 created a financial link. Eichbaum went into a partnership with her brother in a company founded by her father—a printery, papermill, and bindery which produced textbooks and stationery supplies—and then arranged for Alfred Anshutz (1817–1890) to market these products in rural Pennsylvania. When Alfred Anshutz's daughter Margaretta married George Balmain (ca. 1842–?), another generation continued the business association. Both William Eichbaum and Samuel Johnston had other business interests. William Eichbaum was involved in a river navigation enterprise with Thomas and John B. Bakewell in a similar network. Considering the sample size of only twenty families, it is remarkable that their interests, both financial and familial, became so entwined. The connections were even more impressive in view of the fact that William Eichbaum and Eliza Holmes (wife of Alfred Anshutz) were both listed in Powelson's founding families.

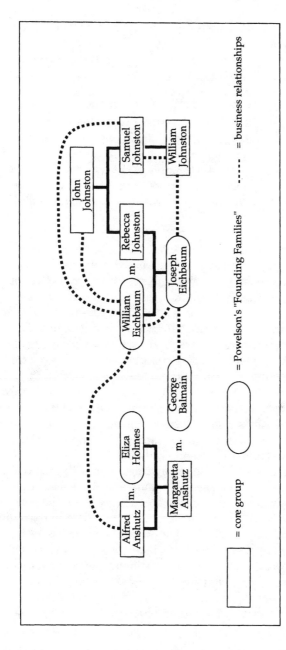

FIGURE 6. A Founding Family Marriage and Business Network

The marital and economic bonds formed networks which facilitated the uninterrupted operation of the accumulation of advantages for each succeeding generation (see figure 4). Non-core males were accepted in both types of relationships, knitting the core families into a single web. This association of families through business and marriage created a pool of capital and expertise. When opportunities presented themselves, family members were able to draw on relatives or business associates for investment capital, management assistance, and, in some cases, advantages in the supply of materials or services from other business ventures. This facilitated far greater achievements for individuals in these families than would have been possible for a single individual acting on his own.

Figure 7 illustrates how inbred the founding families could become. In this rather extreme case, the marriage of two non-core individuals occasioned the partial amalgamation of four core group families in the sample.

The marriage of Asher Phillips (1790–1843) and Sarah Ormsby united two families of similar backgrounds. The family founders arrived in Allegheny County very early, one before and one just after the Revolutionary War. They both had military connections and both were urban in orientation. The Bakewells and Pages also shared a similar background. Both family founders migrated from England at about the same time and set up importing businesses in New York. In fact, it was Elizabeth Page's father's investment in Thomas Bakewell's (1778–1874) father's glasshouse that brought the Page family to Pittsburgh. Mary Phillips's marriage to Hill Burgwin in 1849 was also between partners of equal station. The Burgwins were included in Powelson's index. It can be assumed that Elizabeth Bakewell also married within her class since her daughter, Euphemia James, was considered a suitable marriage partner for Henry Burgwin (1854–1925). It is certainly an indication of the care with which marriage partners were selected that their descendants were eligible for marriage to other founding family descendants.

It can scarcely be overemphasized how dependent found-

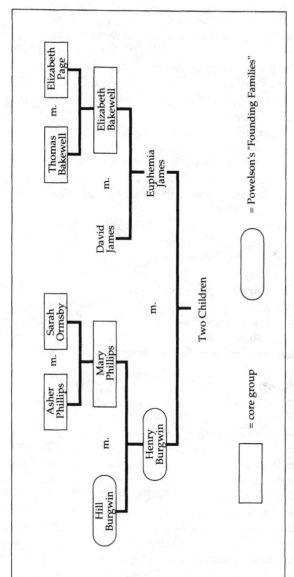

FIGURE 7. Core Family Amalgamation via a Non-core marriage

ing family success was upon the family stability that resulted from intraclass marriages. That economic power was reinforced by ties of marriage is not necessarily, as some historians have alleged, evidence of an insidious attempt on the part of the elite to concentrate economic and probably political power in their own hands and then pass it to their children with the expectation that they do the same. (If this was their goal, they were not too successful, since 25 percent of the group were marginal or unsuccessful.) Instead, the high rate of intermarriage was inevitable, given the tendency of people to seek out others of similar socioeconomic status. This elite, increasingly separated from the population at large, found greater reinforcement of their values and life-styles among members of their own class. The consolidation of economic power was a by-product of this tendency. It is also evident that the formation of family-oriented business associations was, in that precorporation era, motivated more by a desire to rely on "dependable" individuals than by class consciousness. To members of the elite, business relationships and personal relationships were not always clearly distinguished. "Dependable" often meant family, because family members tended to have a stronger sense of commitment to family business enterprises. Emotional attachments reinforced these commitments.

It is perhaps symbolic of the relationship between business and marriage that of the 787 marriages, 20 were known to be between relatives, and some of these were as close as first cousins. James Paxton (1860–1944?) married his first cousin, Helen Jane Paxton. Benjamin L. Fahnestock (1810–1888), after the death of his first wife, married Mary Frances Fahnestock, his first cousin. Occasionally families would be merged by several marriages as when the Hager brothers, Henry (ca. 1858–?) and Frederick (ca. 1849–?) married the Dilworth sisters, Gertrude and Sarah. In one unusual case, three Fahnestock sisters married two brothers and their nephew in the 1870s. Two cousins, each named Robert Knox, married the Liggett sisters, Elizabeth and Isabella, in the 1830s. Although she did not marry a blood relative, Nicholine Ford, daughter of Martha Harding

Page by her first marriage, became the wife of her stepfather's son by his first marriage.

Not all founding family members married, especially the women. Among core group males only seventeen (about seven percent) are known never to have married. No wife is given for another forty-three, and a large percentage of them were probably unmarried. Twelve died before the age of thirty-five, victims of wars, accidents, or disease. Their untimely deaths precluded marriage. The non-core group experienced ten such early deaths.

Of all the males with no recorded wife, only 62 percent were successful. Twenty percent were marginal and 18 percent were unsuccessful. Francis Humes (1846–?), the son of Mary Negley, was a janitor in a railroad yard office at the meridian of his career. William Henry Denny Wilkins (1850–1902) was a bookkeeper for all his working life. Many of the marginally successful or unsuccessful may have actually avoided marriage. Still, the majority of bachelors were successful and many of them were men of prominence with long and illustrious careers. Thomas Bakewell (1792–1866), a bachelor, headed the family glass business. At the same time he was president of the Monongahela Navigation Company, the Monongahela Bridge Company, the Pittsburgh & Connellsville Railroad, and the Pittsburgh Gas Company. His public life was equally remarkable. As president of Pittsburgh's Select Council, he was chosen treasurer of the relief fund following the great fire of 1845. During the Civil War, Bakewell was made a member of the city's Committee of Public Safety and the Sanitary Commission. He also served as president of Pittsburgh's Board of Trade, of Western Pennsylvania Hospital, and as a manager of Western University.

Eighteen percent of the core founding family daughters did not marry. Other than their inheritances, they seldom had any source of income since they did not profit from the family firm except through the largess of other family members. They usually lived with their parents at the family home until their parents died, and then went to live with some other relative. After her father's death, Amelia Brereton's estate was not sufficient to maintain her adequately, so she entered an Episcopalian convent. Others joined their married relatives in volunteer work. Mary Alice Negley was a Red Cross worker, and Alicia Sellers Guthrie was active in organizations serving veterans' hospitals and the center for the blind. Although relatively well educated as a group, few unmarried women pursued careers. Margaret Jane McClure was a teacher and served as librarian for the public library of McKeesport, Pennsylvania. Georgina G. Negley was the first editor of *The Recorder*, published by the Pennsylvania College for Women Alumnae Organization, after her graduation in 1883. Neither of these careers afforded an upper-class life-style, however. Matilda Wilkins Denny was unusual in being wealthy enough to become a philanthropist. She gave family property to Dickinson College where a new campus building was named Denny Hall. Unmarried daughters often occupied their time with the keeping of family records and genealogies. They were not only included, but also well treated, in upper-class biographical publications. Adelaide Nevin's *Social Mirror*, published in 1888, refers to the three unmarried Guthrie women as "prominent in society, and also in charitable work."[7]

Non-core unmarried women generally followed the same pattern as the core women, but there were some notable exceptions. Elizabeth G. Gibson and her sister Matilda Denny Gibson taught school in Chicago. Harriet H. Doughty, daughter of Martha Guthrie, was the only music teacher in the Cincinnati public schools. Elizabeth L. Williams, daughter of Mary Herron, was an exhibiting artist who traveled widely through Europe and taught in San Francisco until her death. An outstanding example of public involvement was Kate Cassatt McKnight, daughter of Elizabeth O'Hara Denny. She was the first woman member of the Pittsburgh School Board, the originator of the free kindergarten system in Allegheny County, and the advocate for juvenile justice who was largely responsible for the passage of juvenile court legislation and the raising of the age limit in child labor legislation. Despite these examples, most of the unmarried women who had prestige but not income led constricted and inward lives close to home.

Children

Founding family marriages provided stable environments for raising children (only two ended in divorce). They also conferred certain advantages on the children. The success of the parents translated into the social class in which they lived and had great impact on their children's lives.

Within the social order, children assume a meaning peculiar to the class to which they are born. In the lower class they are accepted as a consequence of marriage whose labor was needed to maintain the family; in the middle class they are seen as a projection of the parents' personalities into a better future; in the upper class they are valued as carriers of the family heritage and name and are expected to continue family control of the business or profession and keep the family inheritance intact. Because the last of these may best be accomplished if their numbers are not too great, the upper class has tended to have fewer children than any of the other classes.[8]

Among the founding families, children assumed different meanings at different times. In the 1820 period, they were valued as reliable employees whose assistance was needed in getting the family firm established. While family founder George Anshutz manufactured ironware in Huntington County, Pennsylvania, his sons handled the retailing in the western part of the state. Similarly, Oliver Ormsby (1767–1832) managed his father's Pittsburgh-based mercantile business at Erie and Niagara while his brother Joseph (1770–1803) obtained coffee in Jamaica. Benjamin Bakewell's son risked imprisonment in Great Britain when he illegally recruited skilled labor for his father's glasshouse in Pittsburgh. The Gilfillan and Sturgeon children assisted their parents in developing and expanding their landed estates. Daughters too were pressed into service; Rebecca Johnston assisted in running the Pittsburgh post office while her father and later her husband held the office of postmaster.

Although the founding family children were always welcome in the family business, as the nineteenth century reached midpoint and the developmental phase of many of their businesses passed, the average number of children per family declined. This was part of a national trend, and a number of social and demographic influences was responsible.

Table 26 shows how the small family gained in popularity throughout the nineteenth century, mostly at the expense of the very large family. Even in 1820 it constituted a significant proportion of all the families. By 1860 almost half the families had three children or less, and by 1900 this size predominated. The four-to-six-child family was quite common in 1860 but declined greatly by 1900.[9] The greatest change occurred in the decline of the family of seven or more children. The large family, so popular in the 1820 period, had become rare by 1900. It is significant that family sizes, which were evenly distributed in 1820—each category having roughly one-third of the total—became much more uniform by 1900. In this as in other aspects of their lives, the founding families made the transition from great diversity to a condition approaching consensus.

The precipitous decline in the number of children per fam-

TABLE 26
Founding Family Size, 1820–1900[a]

Period	Number of Children						
	3 or less		4 to 6		7 or More		
	%	No.	%	No.	%	No.	Total
1820	32%	(38)	31%	(37)	37%	(45)	120
1860	49	(125)	40	(104)	11	(29)	258
1900	71	(162)	25	(57)	4	(9)	228

a. Includes all children listed in genealogies, biographies, or family histories, even those who did not survive to adulthood. Many who died in infancy were undoubtedly not listed.

ily among the founding families acquires additional meaning when compared to national trends. A variety of statistics exists for the United States, but the most directly comparable measure is the "total fertility rate," the average number of children borne by a woman in her lifetime. Figure 8 compares the average number of children borne by white women between the ages of fourteen and forty-five, regardless of marital state, with founding family statistics. The latter are household figures which include only the married sons and daughters. (Inclusion of the sixty-seven unmarried daughters would have depressed the averages slightly.)

The most outstanding feature for both the founding families and the U.S. population is the enormous decline in the number of children born. The American birth rate fell by nearly one-half over the course of the nineteenth century, as it did among the founding families. However, the founding families had a lower birth rate initially. In 1800 their birth rate was only three-fourths of the national average. By 1900 they were having only 2.85 children per household whereas an average white American woman could expect to have three to four children during her lifetime.[10] Just as they had been ahead of the larger society regarding occupational structure, so too the founding families anticipated the trend toward fewer children. Once again, they were in advance of the general population, in this case by forty to fifty years.

In view of the secular trend toward smaller families, with fewer children to be maintained within the elite upper class, it is remarkable that the success rate of the founding families declined slowly but continuously throughout the nineteenth century. Clearly, factors other than family size influenced their success. Societal and technological changes, competition, migration, the wisdom exercised in selecting a marriage partner, the availability of opportunities, and the ability of later generations to recognize and successfully act upon such opportunities as did exist, all played a role in determining success.

The special status of the first-born male found positive legal and social sanction in European society and, to a limited

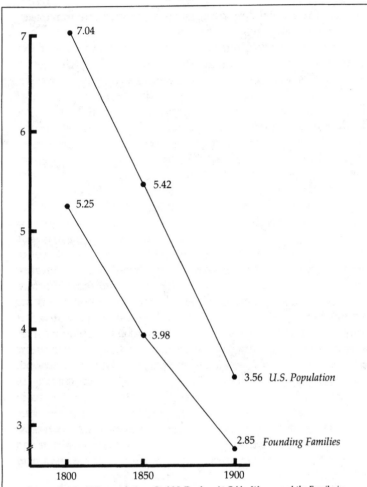

Source: for the U.S. population, Carl N. Degler, *At Odds: Women and the Family in America from the Revolution to the Present* (New York: Oxford University Press, 1980), p. 181.

Note: In 1800 the founding family birth rate was 75 percent of the national average; in 1850 it was 73 percent; and in 1900, 80 percent. The dates 1800, 1850, and 1900 are used in order to compare the founding family data with available national statistics.

FIGURE 8. Number of Children per Founding Family Household Compared to the Number of Children Born to White American Women, 1800, 1850, and 1900

degree, in colonial American society, through the practice of primogeniture.[11] Among the founding families, primogeniture was not practiced, even to a limited extent. No instance was found, in either the eighteenth or the nineteenth centuries, of the eldest son receiving all or even more than his proportional share of the estate relative to the other sons.[12] Nor were daughters excluded from the will, though land was usually willed to the sons, especially among agricultural families. Daughters were more likely to receive down comforters than prime bottom land. By the mid-nineteenth century, however, daughters typically shared equally with sons in the division of family estates.

The rate of success achieved by the children can also be considered in relation to both the size of the family and the individual's chronological order of birth within the family. It is generally believed that the eldest son is more successful in terms of occupational attainment than sons born later because leadership has been required of him since childhood. Supposedly the psychological benefits of childhood responsibility are realized in attainments later in adult life. Correspondingly, it is thought that the childhood resignation of younger sons to inferior status arising from age relationship to the eldest manifests itself in somewhat less outstanding attainments in adulthood.

Among the eldest core group sons, some 69 percent were successful, 23 percent marginally successful, and 8 percent unsuccessful (table 27). But they were no more successful than the core group as a whole and indeed were slightly less successful. (It should be noted, however, that the success rates varied greatly from family to family—all six eldest sons were found

TABLE 27
Success Rates of First-born Sons Compared to
Core Group (N = 418)

	Successful		Marginal		Unsuccessful	
First Son	69%	(91)	23%	(30)	8%	(11)
Core Group	72	(205)	20	(59)	8	(22)

successful in the Liggett family while only six out of fifteen were so classified in the McClure family.) The question then arises, Does the accumulation of advantages work for all elite upper-class sons to much the same degree, regardless of birth order? Or do some of the larger families, with more sons, exercise a proportionately greater effect, thus depressing the average? In most families, considered as equal units, regardless of size, the average of successful first sons does not exceed that of the entire group. Indeed, in seven of the twenty founding families, none of the first sons were marginal or unsuccessful. If each family is counted equally rather than considering the group as an aggregate, a far different result is obtained. In the average family, the percentage of first-born successful sons was 79 percent, considerably higher than the entire group. This inevitably leads to the question, Is the rate of success among the children inversely proportional to family size?

Some founding families had large families; others had small ones. The Brunot, Wrenshall, and Johnston families through all generations in this study had few children. But most of the agricultural families such as Negley, McClure, and Sturgeon (the Gilfillans are an exception) tended to have large families. Thus the total number of individuals descended from or married into each founding family surname differs enormously. The twenty founding families, over all generations studied, may be divided into small—less than twenty people; medium—twenty to fifty people; and large—fifty to eighty-five people. The mean size for each group was twelve, thirty, and sixty-three, respectively. Table 28 shows the success rate of each group. With the exception of one cell (the unsuccessful group of the medium-sized family), the statistics lend support to theories supposing that the amount of success is diluted with increased family size. Perhaps this is a consequence of spreading the accumulation of advantages too thinly. This relationship is shown most dramatically among the small families, where 88 percent of the individuals for whom information is known were ranked as successful as opposed to 65 percent of the individuals in large families. This

TABLE 28
Success Rates by Family Size (N = 609)

Family Size	Successful		Marginal		Unsuccessful	
Small	88%	(53)	5%	(3)	7%	(4)
Medium	78	(281)	17	(62)	5	(16)
Large	65	(124)	25	(48)	10	(18)

difference is inversely paralleled in the marginally successful group. One in four of the members of large families were marginal as compared to only one in twenty among the small families. While the number of unsuccessful was higher for large families than for small families, the percentages do not increase consistently with family size. The percentage of unsuccessful among medium families was slightly smaller than among the small-sized families, though the percentage of unsuccessful was highest among the large families.

The statistics given in table 28 are, of course, averages. Some diversity existed among the various families in terms of success as a function of their size. Figure 9 shows that while there is not a perfect relationship between success and family size, neither has an average been derived from wildly random figures. In fact, even the locus formed by the dots is not a straight line. Because the locus curves slightly upward as family size increases, it could be concluded that while success decreases with increased family size, the rate of success levels off once a certain threshold is reached. A family, regardless of the extreme size attained, will never experience a zero percentage of success. Presumably, it should only drop to a percentage of success approaching that of the total population.

In relating family size to success, some reservations must be made in light of data presented previously. Certainly some relationship existed between family size and success, but its importance should not be overemphasized. Other variables at least as important must have influenced success for the following reason: even as the number of children in founding fami-

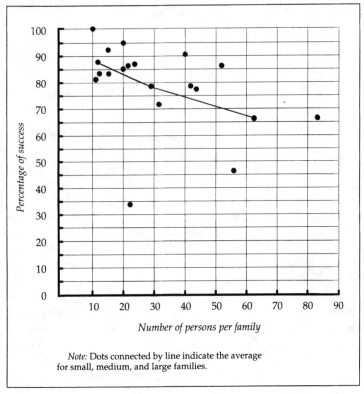

FIGURE 9. Relationship Between Size of Family and the Percentage of Successful in Each Family

lies plummeted 46 percent from the 1820 period to the 1900 period, the percentage of successful as shown in table 7 declined 5 percent instead of increasing, which it would have done were family size the sole determinant of success. Were this the only independent variable, the rate of success would have increased as the size of the nuclear family dropped in each passing generation. Like marriage, family size was but one of many influences on founding family success.

Conclusion

Founding family members were fortunate in the stability of their marriages and the high rates of success of their children. Although the importance of love and luck in choosing a spouse cannot be measured quantitatively, founding family members obviously did not enter into marriage lightly. If they were selective in their club and organizational memberships, they were even more selective when they married. The high percentage of marriages to individuals known to be of equal class and economic level, whether from a local or nonlocal family, attests to their ability to differentiate themselves from the general population and gravitate to their own kind.

Similarly, the number of children born to the founding families was not left completely to chance. They had fewer children in advance of a trend toward smaller families in the general population. This growing consensus in the desired number of offspring among upper-class families perhaps was a response to changing economic situations, changing occupational needs, changing life-styles, and a sincere desire to prepare the young for success with every possible advantage.

VIII

Social Institutions

Religion

"HOWEVER MUCH details may differ, stratification is found in all American communities, and religion is always one of its salient features."[1] So wrote Liston Pope of the Yale Divinity School. Not only do the details of stratification differ, but the social status of religious denominations varies widely from place to place and over time. In the late eighteenth century, the Anglican church made such significant inroads among the upper classes of Quaker Philadelphia and Congregationalist New England, that it was well on its way to becoming the dominant church of the upper classes on the eastern seaboard even though these places were still somewhat isolated from each other.[2] Even in Pittsburgh, where the Scotch-Irish clung tenaciously to their Presbyterian faith, the Episcopalians in the 1820s constituted a small but highly respected group which gained in numbers and prestige throughout the nineteenth century.

Table 29 illustrates the changing religious makeup of the founding families from 1820 to 1900. Although religious data are sparse, the predominance of the Presbyterians is evident in all periods, ranging from 1820, when over two-thirds of the founding family members were adherents to some form of Presbyterianism, to 1900, when a little over a half were so

166

TABLE 29
Founding Family Religious Affiliation, 1820–1900

Religion	1820 (N=66)		1860 (N=132)		1900 (N=127)	
Episcopalian	14%	(9)	21%	(28)	27%	(34)
Presbyterian	60	(39)	50	(66)	52	(66)
Covenanter	2	(1)	1	(1)	—	—
Reformed Presbyterian	3	(2)	2	(2)	—	—
United Presbyterian	3	(2)	13	(17)	3	(4)
Methodist	9	(6)	7	(9)	7	(9)
German Reformed	6	(4)	—	—	—	—
Lutheran	2	(1)	2	(3)	2	(3)
Baptist	—	—	2	(3)	1	(1)
Roman Catholic	2	(1)	2	(3)	5	(6)
Other	2	(1)	—	—	3	(4)

affiliated. The various forms of Presbyterianism were by no means equal in social status. The First Presbyterian Church, in what was to become the city's central business district, was the most prestigious in the county in 1820, and 16 percent of all founding family Presbyterians belonged to that congregation. Despite ongoing outmigration, that congregation still held 7 percent of the founding family Presbyterians in 1900. Membership in the United Presbyterian Church was 13 percent of all founding family members in 1860. However, it was not esteemed by other Presbyterians, and membership fell to 3 percent by 1900. Membership in the doctrinally conservative Covenanter and Reformed Presbyterian churches was never popular, and by the 1900 period no founding family member dared belong to these churches. Although still a majority, the continuous decline in membership experienced by the Presbyterians between 1820 and 1900 was the worst decline suffered by any denomination.

Most of the Presbyterian losses were realized as gains by the Episcopalians. The growth of the Episcopal church among the founding families was evident in each time period. While the gains made by the Episcopal church lagged behind its growth among the upper classes in eastern cities, it had managed to attract more than a fourth of the founding family members by 1900. Such an increase in the face of strong Presbyterian resistance was ample evidence of the degree to which the founding families were absorbed into a national upper class which itself was becoming more Episcopalian.

Despite their smaller numbers, the Episcopalians made strong efforts in Allegheny County to match Presbyterian accomplishments in establishing church-related institutions. In 1854 for example, the Pittsburgh Female College was established by the Presbyterian church. Clearly it was intended as an institution for educating the daughters of the wealthy. Rather than witness the defection of its younger members, the Episcopalian church countered with the Bishop Bowman Institute, established in 1862 ostensibly for the daughters of good Episcopalians although it accepted students from other faiths as well.

Upon analysis of table 29, it might be concluded that in terms of religion, considerable consensus existed among the founding families in all periods. Yet if the statistics are interpreted differently, an even greater tendency toward consensus may be discerned. If we combine the figures for all the Protestant denominations that were not upper class—Covenanter, Reformed Presbyterian, Methodist, Baptist, German Reformed, and Lutheran (Roman Catholicism is excluded because it had no hopes of becoming an upper-class religion in nineteenth-century America outside a few strongholds such as Baltimore and New Orleans)—the downward trend of membership in churches with less wealthy and less educated congregations is unmistakable, from 22 percent in 1820 to 14 percent in 1860, to 10 percent in 1900.

The losses experienced by the ethnic-associated churches were the most pointed. Assimilation into the upper class mandated "losing" one's foreignness, and foreignness as manifested in religious affiliation was a major expression of ethnicity. Thus George Senft (1849–1885), son of a German immigrant, was raised a Lutheran, but upon his marriage to

Keziah Negley he became a Presbyterian. Almost always when a conversion occurred it was in the direction of a church with higher social status. Higher social status often meant less foreign, but it need not involve abandoning doctrinal orientation, simply anglicizing it a bit. John H. Negley (1823–1908), whose father had founded the Lutheran church in Butler, Pennsylvania, left that church "in early manhood" but not the doctrines of Lutheranism. Instead, he joined the English Lutheran church. At least one other non-core male who married a Negley did the same. Perhaps two trends were at work, one of Americanization and the other, consequent to it, a step toward consensus among the founding families.

In the first half of the nineteenth century Methodists and Baptists were becoming integrated into the American middle class, though a reservoir of hostility toward them continued. When Mary Ann Gilfillan McBride, wife of James McBride (1798–?), moved to Indiana with her husband and children, she wrote home in 1846 complaining, "We do not enjoy the happiness of good society, we live among Baptists."[3] Perhaps the Baptists were too much to bear, since the McBrides later moved to Wisconsin.

Later in the century Florence Dilworth, whose husband DeWitt Dilworth (1853–?) was prominent and prosperous, lived on fashionable Aiken Avenue in Pittsburgh's East End. She helped organize the First Church of Christ Scientist in Pittsburgh. She was not included in Nevin's *Social Mirror* though she was an appropriate thirty-one years of age when the book was published in 1888. She possessed all the other entrance requirements, and other Dilworth women were included. Her only son was raised as a Christian Scientist but her husband, resisting all her entreaties, refused to join.

In some instances the founding family members even left Presbyterianism when it became too "enthusiastic." Such was the case of family founder Alexander Gilfillan who was a member of Bethel Presbyterian Church in southern Allegheny County during a period of religious frenzy. The 1802 revival "was accompanied by some rather extreme emotional disturbances—people falling to the ground unable to speak." The consequent effect on Alexander "was to cause him to withdraw from Bethel and to join in forming a church of the Associate Reform branch of the Presbyterian faith." He became an elder of the new church, but his wife, Martha Gilfillan, retained her membership at Bethel. When he died in 1836, Martha had the last word and had him buried at Bethel. Alexander's son, John Gilfillan (1785–1859), trying to avoid the conflict, held membership in both churches. Alexander's second son, Andrew Gilfillan (1790–1873), was a trustee at Bethel, but the entire family still living in the area (all of the daughters had married and moved) converted to the Associate Reformed church following Martha's death in 1840.[4]

Despite the liturgical features that Roman Catholics shared with Episcopalians, upper-class social lines were firmly drawn against them. It has been noted how Dr. Felix Brunot abandoned his Catholicism in order to be accepted into the ranks of Pittsburgh's best families. While Brunot did become an Episcopalian, William Eichbaum, also once a Catholic, was not quite willing to embrace Protestantism. In describing his religion, Eichbaum's biographer wrote simply, "private devotion."

Despite a Presbyterian background, the Dennys were the most tolerant of Catholicism of all the founding families. William Irwin Denny (1840–?) married a Catholic although he himself never converted. His biographer lamented that William "died when his twin children were very small and they were reared as Catholics;" however, their Catholic education was due to the influence of another Denny, not their mother's family.[5] They were educated by William's cousin, Harmer Denny (1834–1908), who did convert to Catholicism and became a Jesuit. The Dennys' acceptance of Catholicism was shown in the fact that he was neither disowned nor disinherited as Reuben Sturgeon had been in 1813. Denny became the secretary of Cardinal Manning, rising from a new convert to a position, if not at the pinnacle of power itself, at power's right hand. Further proof of the Denny acceptance of Catholicism is that at least one other of Harmer's cousins, Ebenezer Denny Harding (1830–1868), sent his daughter to Ursaline Academy, a Roman Catholic girls' school, although the family was not Catholic.

The rest of the founding families were ready to resist incursions by Catholics into any level of society. Writing of Rev. David C. Page (1801–1878), an Episcopal minister, Benjamin G. Bakewell in 1892 rejoiced that "he went to Natchez to replace the pastor who had joined the 'Roman Church.' By the efforts of Dr. Page, not a member of the Natchez congregation followed the errant pastor."[6]

At times, however, class consciousness did overcome religious antagonisms. William G. Johnston (1828–1913) left memoirs in which he was still nursing wounds inflicted on the Scottish Presbyterians in the seventeenth century by the Stuart monarchs whom he described as "miserable tools" of "papal power." Though he inveighed against the papacy on more than one occasion, William Johnston did not vote for the anti-Catholic candidate in Pittsburgh's mayoralty election of 1850. In the election, the lower-class, fist-swinging Joseph Barker successfully ran for office from a jail cell. He had been arrested for inciting an anti-Catholic riot in front of St. Patrick's Church in Pittsburgh. Barker, who "had a large following, especially among working-class Protestants," also "directed his harangues against . . . the economic elite."[7] In a personal contest pitching intense religious loyalties against those of class, Johnston chose to vote for a fellow founding family member, John B. Guthrie (1807–1885). Either class counted more than religion, or this member of the elite upper class, while he may have been anti-Catholic, was not willing to vent his feelings through one as unrefined as Barker or to vote for someone opposed to the economic elite.

Possibly the founding families attached less importance to religious affiliation at the end of the nineteenth century than they did earlier. Perhaps the fact that church membership was less apt to be recorded in the 1900 period than the 1860 period is an indication of this. Family genealogies and biographical encyclopedias included information on religion less frequently in the early twentieth century than they had in the nineteenth. Despite the rising population of founding family members, the number for whom church membership could be found actually declined between 1860 and 1900. While the volume of available occupational data increased 137 percent between 1820 and 1900, in that same time span the volume of church membership data increased only 92 percent. If this indicates increased secularization, then the founding families were, in this respect, little different from the larger society. By 1900 club memberships had replaced church memberships as important indicators of upper-class status. And this was joined by yet another indicator, education.

Education

Believing it was the quality of education and the skills learned which were partly responsible for maintaining the upper class in a position of economic dominance, Gabriel Kolko, student of social class structure and income inequality, wrote that "higher education at the best institutions perpetuates the advantages of wealth in succeeding generations."[8] This may be true, but perhaps not in the sense intended by Kolko. It was not true that education per se at the best institutions perpetuated the advantages of wealth. The social interactions occurring in those institutions far outweighed the educational process as a factor in the perpetuation of upper-class dominance. They created an atmosphere, much in the manner of a social club, for the maintenance of the social ties that already bound members of their class together. Partly because noneducational aspects of student life were typically paramount for the upper class, education per se was not a vehicle for either economic or social upward mobility. The role of extraeducational activities was underscored by one genealogist perhaps more than even he realized. Writing of the educational career of James O'Hara Denny (1855–1921), the only comment made was that he got the longest hit ever made by the Princeton baseball team.[9]

Among the founding families there were, of course, many

whose academic achievements were notable. But there was also a sizable proportion who never attended either college or high school and for whom the socialization process occurred outside formal educational institutions (see table 30). Much data is missing because in instances where little formal education was acquired, education tended not to be mentioned in the sources. Yet in later time periods when education, at least to the high-school level, was far more prevalent, the lack of information may be due to the assumption that everyone was so educated. The definition of what constituted a complete education changed as the average number of years of education increased with each succeeding generation. The importance of education and its availability changed through the time periods and therefore the reasons for the failure to record such data also changes. Table 30 does, however, show a trend toward more education, especially in the precipitous decline in the "negligible" category as lack of education became more uncommon and worthy of note. The percentage of non-college-educated founding family members probably declined about 40 percentage points from 1820 to 1900.

The location of the colleges and universities attended by founding family members changed considerably over time (see table 31). Much of the data for 1820 reflects education obtained prior to arrival in Allegheny County. All those obtaining a foreign education in this period did so before emigrating to the United States. This is not true of succeeding periods, but sending their children abroad was never as popular among the

TABLE 30
Non-College Founding Family Members as a Proportion of the Total for Whom Education Is Known (N=98)

Amount of Education	1820		1860		1900	
Negligible	39%	(25)	9%	(11)	1%	(2)
Grade school	11	(7)	16	(21)	6	(9)
High school	6	(4)	7	(9)	7	(10)
% Non-college	56		32		14	

TABLE 31
Colleges Attended, 1820–1900

College or Area	1820 (N=29)		1860 (N=89)		1900 (N=126)	
Western University of Pennsylvania[a]	7%[f]	(2)	13%	(12)	14%	(18)
Pittsburgh area	3	(1)	7	(6)	8	(10)
Washington & Jefferson[b]	3	(1)	16	(14)	4	(5)
Tri-state area[c]	3	(1)	3	(3)	2	(2)
In Pennsylvania[d]	14	(4)	7	(6)	5	(7)
Harvard or Yale	3	(1)	7	(6)	5	(7)
Princeton	3	(1)	3	(3)	13	(16)
Other Ivy League[e]	3	(1)	4	(4)	8	(10)
Eastern U.S.	10	(3)	13	(12)	9	(12)
Southern U.S.	—	—	2	(2)	2	(3)
West or Midwest	—	—	1	(1)	7	(9)
Foreign	17	(5)	2	(2)	2	(3)
Unspecified	31	(9)	20	(18)	19	(24)

a. University of Pittsburgh
b. Washington and Jefferson were separate colleges until 1865.
c. Wooster, Bethany, etc.
d. Allegheny, Dickinson, etc., excluding the University of Pennsylvania.
e. University of Pennsylvania, Cornell, etc.
f. Percentages do not equal 100 due to rounding.

founding families as it was reputed to have been among the eastern elite, especially during the Gilded Age.

Most often the founding families chose to educate their children close to home. In 1820, 31 percent of the college-educated founding family members were locally educated; by 1860 this figure had increased to 46 percent. In 1900, however, it declined to only 33 percent. It is significant that the peak in local education was reached at mid-century rather than earlier. Operating here were two trends of integration, the integration of the local upper class, followed by the nationalization of the upper class. Local upper classes had to develop a definition of their own identity, and an agreed upon understanding of who was to be included before a national upper class could be established. This phenomenon was not unique to Allegheny County by any means. Prior to the Civil War, the largely separated local upper classes were educated within their respective states.

The Western University of Pennsylvania (rechartered as the University of Pittsburgh in 1908) was the most frequently attended local institution of higher learning. It claimed only 7 percent of the college-educated founding family members in 1820, but this percentage grew to 14 in 1860 and stayed at that level through 1900. Washington College in Washington, Pennsylvania, and Jefferson College in nearby Canonsburg merged as Washington and Jefferson College in 1865. At that time these two institutions combined had been chosen by 16 percent of the founding families' college-age children. It was especially favored by those families residing south of Pittsburgh. No clear consensus regarding a preferred local school existed in the 1860 period. Families sent their children to a wide variety of schools in the city of Pittsburgh, the tri-state area (continguous regions of Pennsylvania, Ohio, and West Virginia), or elsewhere in western or central Pennsylvania. Although Washington and Jefferson suffered a serious decline around 1900, probably as a result of nationalizing trends in education, founding families still continued to send a substantial number of their college-aged children to local schools.

After the Civil War, the American upper class started to flock to what was to become known as the "big three"—Harvard, Yale, and Princeton.[10] The founding families participated in this trend only to a limited degree since Western Pennsylvanians found little social acceptance among the upper class of the eastern seaboard. Excluded from many of the elite clubs, fraternities, and societies, they felt denied the social contacts and ambiance that they expected at an upper class school. Attendance at Harvard, Yale, and Princeton, rose from 10 percent in the 1860 period to over 18 percent in the 1900 period. Princeton was the most favored by the founding families, as it would be by the sons of Pittsburgh's post–Civil War iron and steel elite.[11] Other Ivy League schools also experienced a significant rise as a part of the early trend toward the formation of a nationally recognized upper class.

The education obtained by the elder and younger Kerrs typified this trend away from localism. In 1834 Rev. John Kerr graduated from Washington College, located in the same county in which he was born. His son, however, born in Monongahela City (later Pittsburgh's South Side), graduated from Princeton in 1878. Implicit here is the establishment of contacts over a wider geographical and, therefore, psychological area as a part of intergenerational development. Perhaps it is symbolic of their respective range of contacts that while the elder Kerr died at Indian Run, Pennsylvania, less than forty miles from his birthplace, his son died in California.

The statistics on college attendance at local institutions in table 31 incorporate some nonlocal students from founding families who moved away from Allegheny County. Many of these families retained strong ties with the area and sent their children back to be educated with friends and relatives where the family reputation gained them immediate social acceptance. Founding family migrants were influenced by the same forces toward nationalization as their Allegheny County relatives, but participated in the movement toward the Ivy League schools to an even greater degree since they were less tied to place. Their inclusion in table 31, however, accounts for much of the attendance at non–Ivy League eastern, southern, midwestern, and western schools which for them were local institutions.

The trend toward a national upper class with universally recognized educational institutions was part of a far greater integrating phenomenon. At the same time that young upper-class men and women were associating with others of their kind from different areas at prestigious institutions, their elder brothers and sisters were choosing spouses from the same group: upper class and nonlocal. The trends grew simultaneously and reinforced each other. Nonlocal colleges served as vehicles for meeting nonlocal, upper-class marriage partners, and the connections formed by these marriages drew other family members to nonlocal schools. These associations in turn helped strengthen and nationalize business connections. Combined with a growing corporate network, the push toward nationalization of the upper class was strong indeed.

Among the founding families, as within the larger society, education and occupation were related. Table 32 shows the increase in the percentage of college-educated founding family members in each time period over the previous period. Even in the 1820 period the percentage of all those for whom occupation was known who were college educated was high at 25 percent. By the 1860 period this had risen to 34 percent and by 1900 to 43 percent.

Understandably, in every period the professionals were the most educated group. Aside from a negligible change among clerks and laborers, they were the only group to experience a decline in the percentage of college-educated (in 1860). It is certainly possible that this mid-century decline was a manifestation of the Jacksonian "democratization" of the professions whereby less educational preparation was required. More surprising are the figures for manufacturing and mining (23 percent college educated in 1900), which contradict the popular myth of the self-made, uneducated industrialist as typified by Andrew Carnegie. The same was true of farmers. The percentage of college-educated farmers did not increase greatly in any time period, nor was their number very large, but a rate of more than one in ten, even in 1820, is relatively high. Although college attendance was more common among urbanites, some families, such as the McClures and Nevilles, imitated the life-style of the English rural gentry. These college-educated farmers conceived of themselves more as rural landholders than as agriculturalists.

College education was obviously not a prerequisite for success in some occupational categories, and yet many founding families considered higher education an important part of their children's upbringing. Especially for rural families, socialization through the extracurricular activities attendant to college life drew them into the upper class. Along with marriage, higher education facilitated the homogenization of rural and urban founding families. Rural families experienced

TABLE 32
Occupations of College-Educated Founding Family Members as a Percentage of the Total in Each Category

	1820			1860			1900		
	%	Total	College	%	Total	College	%	Total	College
Professional	81	16	13	74	54	40	85	66	56
Commerce/business	16	25	4	24	66	16	33	108	36
Manufacturing/mining	0	9	0	17	36	6	23	30	7
Government official	29	17	5	42	24	10	73	15	11
Farmer	10	29	3	11	27	3	17	12	2
Clerk/laborer	0	3	0	10	10	1	0	23	0
Military	25	12	3	30	27	8	33	9	3
Total	25	111	28	34	244	84	44	263	115

the greater change as college education served as an agent in their increased urbanization. Many who left the land pursued a profession and took up residence in the city. George A. Gilfillan, for example, was born on the family homestead in Upper Saint Clair Township, Pennsylvania, in 1869. Upon gaining a degree in civil engineering, he moved to Pittsburgh's fashionable South Highland Avenue. In 1901 he was pictured in *Notable Men* and listed as a civil and consulting engineer.[12] Gilfillan is perhaps symbolic of the growing similarity of the rural and urban founding families, who were both gravitating to professional careers. The effect of the college milieu in widening the outlook and interests of the rural founding families served to draw them into urban-oriented networks and helped integrate them into the upper class.

The founding families were correct in their assumption that formal college training would increase their children's chances of success. They were equally correct in assuming that the associations and social interactions that accompanied college life would be as beneficial as classroom instruction. Attendance at a recognized educational institution would later serve as a bond in the formation of a national upper class.

Clubs

By the end of the nineteenth century, a host of social clubs had been established which had the effect of sorting the upper class from the general population, and they did it more precisely than universities or churches ever could. Memberships in these clubs had broader social ramifications than they had in the 1820 period. The small organizations of the earlier periods—the Humane Society or the Chemical and Physiological Society—were ostensibly based on the mutual interests of their members. Membership was not predicated upon social class, although most of the members were of the upper class. Later social clubs and country clubs had broader interests but more closely guarded entrance requirements. To be accepted for membership at the turn of the century was an indicator of upper-class status. Although most of these clubs had significance only in their local areas, some did gain national reputations. Therefore it was not unusual for an upper-class Pittsburgher to belong to prestigious clubs in other cities as well as in Pittsburgh. Out-of-town memberships were even more reliable indicators of entrance into a national upper class and signified social acceptance outside of the local environments.[13]

This transition in the organization and significance of clubs over the course of the nineteenth century can be seen in the Page family history. The family founder, Benjamin Page, was a manager in both the Pittsburgh Permanent Library Association and the Pittsburgh Bible Society. Both organizations were small, local in character, and limited in interest. No club affiliations could be found for his son, John Harding Page (1804–1871), or for his grandson, Benjamin Page, Jr. (1830–1874), although the latter was an incorporator of the YMCA of Pittsburgh in 1869. The great-grandson, however, also named Benjamin Page (1868–1935), was a member of the upper-class Duquesne Club, University Club, Pittsburgh Golf Club, Pittsburgh Athletic Association, and Fox Chapel Golf Club, as well as the Bankers Club of New York City. These four generations were quite typical of the founding families. The family founder exhibited high visibility in his participation in local organizations. His son, educated at Buffalo Seminary (Bethany College), to which "boys from the best Pittsburgh families were sent," was active in "benevolent work" and in the improvement of jails, but he did not hold a single club membership in the traditional sense.[14] In the 1860s, elite upper-class families performed their civic duty in some form of public betterment.[15] In supporting a community effort, they met and associated with others of similar social standing. In many respects the Civil War was a high water mark of this form of associational membership. The founding families threw themselves unreservedly into the organization of Sanitary Fairs (predecessors to the Red Cross) and other war relief efforts.[16] Less than three decades after the war, however, the founding families would be much transformed by the advent of the social club that henceforth characterized the American upper class. The formalized system for identifying social class became the supreme authority in determining the "right" people for inclusion in the upper class. Even after the death of Benjamin Page, Jr., in 1874, his wife and children were considered to be among that group of "right" people since they were included in the first Pittsburgh Blue Book (1889).

The number of social clubs that his son, Benjamin Page, belonged to was certainly impressive. When social clubs established themselves, the upper classes flocked to them as if in competition to see who could amass the most memberships.[17] With time the founding families sorted out the most prestigious and ignored those that were less selective in their memberships. Francis Sellers Guthrie (1869–1936) belonged to the Loyal Legion, the Sons of the American Revolution, the Duquesne Club, the Fox Chapel Golf Club, the Pittsburgh Club, the Pittsburgh Golf Club, the Rolling Rock Country Club, the Army-Navy Club of America, and the Masons, along with a number of professional and civic associations. There were others who had even more club memberships, but Guthrie was careful in his selection.

Mention must be made of the Freemasons, whose members included some of the most notable families in Allegheny county and the nation throughout the nineteenth century. Moreover, membership in the Masons could be transferred through a nationwide network of chapters. This, too, played a part in the accumulation of advantages because it led to the formation of advantageous associations. Participation in the Masons was an introduction to influential businessmen and professionals. All the founding families had Masonic ties, and for some, participation was almost a full-time career. William G. Liggett (1872–1923) was a member of the Blue Lodge Crescent; the Shiloh Chapter of the Royal Arch Masons; the Tancred Commandery of the Knights Templar; the Pennsylvania Consistory; Scottish Rite, Syria Temple; and the Ancient Arabic Order Nobles of the Mystic Shrine.[18] The Masonic orders are of interest to this study in that their nationwide network of chapters far and away preceded that of any other secular organization.

Conclusion

The division of the population along social lines, be it by religion, education, social compatibility, or residential proximity, effects a growing separation from the rest of the population and a consequent increasing homogeneity within the various groups. Whatever the context, social interaction results in something shared by the members of the group which is not shared by those outside the group, thus creating a bond among the members. This interaction solidifies the relationships and reinforces commonly held values.

Social institutions were of great importance to the lives and fortunes of the founding families of Allegheny County. They were not merely outlets for leisure-time recreation; they were an integral part of daily life. Most important, they served as effective means of maintaining the family position. The importance of the various types of social interactions differed according to time periods and family circumstances, but each enhanced and strengthened the family's social ranking and enabled the family to form associations that could be utilized immediately or passed on as advantages to subsequent generations.

Upper-class social position brought with it a respectable and comfortable standard of living, but the primary concern was economic. The founding families had prospered, and a few had accumulated or inherited considerable fortunes, but the life-styles these fortunes permitted had to be maintained and future generations needed the skill to sustain the family fortune. Undeniably this was a major factor in a family's decision to send a child to college and probably an important factor in selecting that college. The founding families had the foresight to realize that college was more than an education and that the social associations formed at college could be translated into economic advantages. The members of the Harvard, Yale, Princeton Club spoke of more than their college days within their clubs in Pittsburgh or any other major city. The business and professional connections renewed and reinforced there could possibly bear economic fruit.

Even membership in social clubs and country clubs had economic ramifications. By establishing a tradition of participation in upper-class clubs, the families protected themselves from a precipitous decline. Even if their fortunes should dwindle, their acceptance as social equals, if they could afford the expense of fees and the outward trappings of success, kept the avenues to profitable associations open. It was through channels such as these that opportunities to renew their economic prominence might arise. Even if the family fortune should not recover, social acceptance was an advantage from which their children might be able to profit.

The religious, educational, or social organizations that had helped to maintain founding family position in the 1900s had their counterparts, although smaller in scale, in the 1820s. Associations with wealthy and influential people offered opportunities to the rising individual who could impress others with his abilities on a personal level. Friendships thus initiated led to introductions to wider circles in an increasing network of associations. In the 1900 period, relationships among the members of a church congregation, college, or club still led to advantageous personal associations. However, with the development of a national upper class, the organization itself acquired an identity and reputation through which members achieved stature outside the community in which they lived.

IX

Conclusion

THIS STUDY of a sample of Allegheny County's earliest elite families and their descendants throughout the nineteenth century traces the degree to which they formed a cohesive upper class. The founders of these families were not the extremely wealthy merchants of eastern cities, nor were they the incredibly rich iron and steel elite of the late nineteenth century for which Pittsburgh became famous. Unlike their eastern contemporaries or their industrial successors, the estates they amassed were not sufficiently large to maintain succeeding generations. These founders started out as a pioneering elite in a western community separated by the mountains from the large cities of the eastern seaboard. In this sense they truly were founding families in a still sparsely populated area with correspondingly limited economic opportunities.

The twenty-four family founders came from distinctive and quite separate economic and cultural backgrounds. They represented a wide range of ethnicities, religions, ages, and socioeconomic origins. These family founders were perhaps as varied an elite as ever characterized an American preindustrial community. Yet they were really no more heterogeneous than the rest of the population, for it too was culturally and economically mixed. Although they all were to become members of the functional elite in Allegheny County, in most other respects the family founders were a microcosm of the general population. Over the period encompassed by this study, their descendants developed similar characteristics in an increasingly diverse society.

The family founders' specific reasons for migrating to Allegheny County may have differed, but their motives were much the same. They had come to realize the main chance, to take advantage of new opportunities for economic success. Inasmuch as they were all in pursuit of the main chance, they had several important characteristics in common, but most particularly, they possessed a driving ambition combined with the readiness to discern and take advantage of new opportunities. The methods they employed in achieving success were very different. Some came with capital to invest in manufacturing or commercial concerns. Others came with little more than the deeds to land grants given them because of their military service. And still others came with only the skills of their occupation. These initial starts, varied though they were, provided a foundation on which their fortunes could be built.

The road to success for the family founders and their immediate descendants was most often found through diversification. In the 1820 period and earlier, diversification manifested itself in the creation of numerous business ventures, small in scale and frequently unrelated to one another. They tended to be speculative, yielding a temporary profit, but without long-term plans for organized growth. Although such short-lived ventures involved a high degree of risk, failure in any one of them did not necessarily bring ruin. The stakes in each venture were small. The lack of structure and interdependence among these enterprises was due to the nature of the interpersonal relationships that characterized the period. Resulting largely from the existing state of preindustrial transportation and communication technologies, these ventures were dependent on relatives and long-standing acquaintances both inside and outside formal organized relationships. Knowing the personal character of a business associate was as important as the business venture itself.

Migration too was largely based on personal relationships

and hearsay concerning opportunities elsewhere. Much like the family founders, the migrants of the 1820 period left in pursuit of the main chance. The risks of failure in a new place were exceedingly high, paralleling the risks in business and life itself. (Given their diet, the state of medicine, and the hazards and hardships they endured, life was truly a gamble.) Like business, migration was often seen as a vehicle for short-term gain, and the pattern of migration was repeated with each new venture.

The ephemeral character of business and migration may have served the founding families well in 1820, but by 1860 more permanence and more structure were required. The smallness, the dependence on friends and relatives, and the speculative aspects of earlier formulas for success were becoming obsolete. The 1860s were transitional in the development of the structure that was so necessary by 1900.

Population growth and the introduction of new technologies rendered ineffective the earlier methods through which the founding families maintained themselves within the elite upper class. A far more elaborate pattern was required to reckon with the changes that were everywhere taking place. This pattern took the form of a more definitive structure. To bring order to an enlarged world, systems were instituted on a variety of levels to formalize and clarify relationships and to specify fields of operation. The new business and social organizations varied greatly in their scope and purpose, ranging from the nationwide corporation with local offices to the locally based clubs affiliated with national organizations. All these bureaucracies made possible the management of masses of people, material, and information. Just as a single person could no longer oversee the growth of many diverse enterprises, all organizations found it necessary to specialize and centralize their activities.

This structure and the large-scale systems which it fostered may have made life more predictable and therefore less risky, but the stakes were now much higher. A single failure could be economically disastrous for founding family members. Although more technological and social change occurred during the nineteenth century than in any previous century, the founding families realized a surprisingly stable success rate. This consistency is explained through the trade-off that was occurring gradually throughout the 1800s. The founding families were giving up diversity for bureaucratized structure, and both proved efficient in maintaining them.

This structure not only paralleled the evolution of an integrated American economy, it was the essence of that integration. And the founding families were not merely reacting to the changes, they actually initiated some of them. The founding families, or at least the more successful among them, were a positive force for change.

The evolution of bureaucratized structure has been most noted in the economic sphere: in manufacturing, transportation, and commerce. These sectors of the economy were the earliest to evolve large-scale structure. The organizational and operational form was the corporation. The founding families participated in the organizational restructuring of business and relied on it to maintain themselves. Founding family members were able to ensconce themselves in executive positions within the rapidly growing national corporations.

For the founding families and the rest of the upper class, structure influenced more than their economic endeavors. Increasingly, structure was applied, perhaps unconsciously, to their social interactions, which previously had rested solely on personal relationships. It developed from a formalization of group consensus and was applied to every type of social institution, identifying certain churches, schools, clubs, and organizations as upper class. As the upper class gradually reached agreement concerning which organizations were the most prestigious, membership in those organizations became almost synonymous with upper-class status. Group consensus was not arrived at for its own sake, however. It was related to the process by which the founding families and the whole American upper class differentiated themselves from the rest of the population. Consensus was neither necessary nor possible in the 1820 period when the social system was built on personal relationships. A family founder and his children may have been highly visible socially as German Lutherans, but they felt little pressure to abandon these ties. By midcentury, however, the entire system, including the number of people in it, was growing enormously. And technological changes of historic proportions were occurring. If the individual founding families were not to be lost in this, they would have to be identifiable not only by the society at large but, most important, recognized by one another. The vehicle by which group identity was developed was marriage. If the descendants of a German Lutheran family founder intermarried with those of a Scotch-Irish Presbyterian family founder, some form of accommodation had to be made. With time it was. By the 1900 period much intermarriage had occurred within the founding families and they had achieved a very notable degree of consensus. They had largely agreed upon the neighborhood to live in, the churches and clubs to join, and the schools their children should attend. They even agreed on how many children they should have.

The occupations which the founding families pursued paralleled this increasing consensus. By the 1900 period, just three occupational categories (professional, finance, and business executive) accounted for about 60 percent of all founding family employment. In 1820 those same three categories had accounted for only 18 percent. In that early period a different set of occupations had attracted the founding families. Even the three most popular nonagricultural occupations (government official, merchant, and professional) had drawn only 38 percent of founding family members. While agriculture was the most popular of all occupations in the 1820 period, it and other frequently chosen occupations (government official is an exception) reflected the lack of large-scale structure in the economic system. They were the very essence of that smallness of scale wherein a single individual could effectively function.

The consensus achieved by 1900 was possible not only because several generations had elapsed since the family founder, but because intermarriage had brought about a sameness of kind. This consensus was not only possible, it was necessary, due to the increased size of the population and the

systems developed to cope with it. It was no longer possible for
the upper class of a city to know every individual within its
group. Nor was it possible for every prominent surname to be
recognized outside of the city in which the family was established. In order for elite society to retain its identity, it was
necessary to create formalized indicators of status. The country
club and, to a limited extent, the parish, served as status indicators on a local level, while universities and religious denominations partially performed this function for the national upper
class. The increase of nonlocal marriages for the founding families from 51 percent in the first two decades of the nineteenth
century to nearly 80 percent after 1880 suggests the growing
need for a reliable means of recognizing members of the same
class in a nonlocal context. Thus a national group consensus
was developed in a much-elaborated social network.

In view of the many changes occurring within the larger
society, it was inevitable that the founding families and the
American upper class would reach consensus in those important aspects of life which would differentiate them from the
rest of the population. It was only natural that they would
seek out those with whom they felt most comfortable, those
who shared their values and life-styles. Before 1800 founding
family members tended to intermarry. But increasingly thereafter, they were dependent upon universally accepted social
status indicators in selecting compatible mates from a national
upper class, that is, mates who shared characteristics by
which the upper class has been traditionally identified.

Even as the founding families were gradually moving toward homogeneity, the larger society was becoming more diverse. To contemporaries, the population of Allegheny County
in 1820 seemed quite varied, representing many religions and a
dozen ethnic groups. An inhabitant of Pittsburgh in 1900, however, would have perceived this same 1820 population as almost homogeneous by comparison. The urbanization that accompanied America's industrialization witnessed an influx of
immigrant laborers who were unlike the older residents.

Allegheny County had become highly urbanized, and
Pittsburgh was the most industrialized city of its size in the

United States. The businesses of the founding families, along with those of other capitalists, had created a demand for laborers on a massive scale. These demands were met by Eastern and Southern Europeans who were predominantly Roman Catholic, Jewish, and Eastern Orthodox. Clustered in ethnic neighborhoods and bonded by their Old World religions, these groups radically changed the makeup of the city's population. Their cultural diversity was more than Pittsburgh could assimilate, at least for the time being. The undesirable jobs and extremely low wages they received reinforced their social separateness. Moreover, social barriers prevented the upward occupational mobility open to the native, old stock, Protestant population. Those same social barriers provided an invisible floor beneath which the old stock Americans rarely sank. Thus by 1900, the founding families, undeniably all old stock by then, occupied positions in a socioeconomic population pyramid twenty-two times larger than it had been in 1820 and buoyed by a mass of immigrants at the bottom.

If the low incomes received by the immigrant laborers attracted the attentions only of Progressive Era reformers, the spectacular fortunes of Carnegie, Frick, the Mellons, Heinz, and Westinghouse were the objects of near universal interest and publicity. The maldistribution of income had reached extremes beyond what had existed in 1820. The founding families neither sank to the economic depths, nor were they among the industrial millionaires. Such celebrated names as Carnegie and Westinghouse, who amassed their fortunes after the Civil War, were not drawn from among the ranks of the founding families. Even the more successful founding family members did not generally maintain the same relative position within Allegheny County's economic pyramid that the family founders enjoyed. That pyramid had grown exponentially in the nineteenth century with the creation of enormous personal fortunes and giant corporations. Yet the founding families had realized a measure of similarity in the level of income which was given tangible expression when they ensconced themselves in the upper-middle to lower-upper-class homes of Pittsburgh's East End or its counterparts in other cities to which they had migrated. This similarity certainly did not embrace all the founding family descendants or even all the successful, since some of them barely escaped a marginally successful existence while others were clearly quite wealthy. However, the similar homes, church memberships, schools, clubs, and other class-associated shibboleths formed the life-style of a clearly identifiable group and helped determine its membership, since a substantial income was required in order to belong. By 1900, the vast majority of the founding family members still received this requisite threshold income.

This similarity was underscored and supported by the founding families' occupational distribution. They increasingly engaged in those occupations considered to be roughly equal in social class status. Whereas the wholesale grocer, the independent lawyer, and the iron manufacturer of 1820 differed markedly from each other in the external appearances of their various occupations, by 1900 the same mahogany desk suited all three for by this time they were all businessmen cast in the role of the stereotypical executive. Although the total number of specific occupations in America had increased greatly as a result of nineteenth-century technological advances, the business executive evolved as a uniform type. By 1900 the managers of manufacturing firms, bankers and other men of commerce, as well as professionals, were largely indistinguishable from one another in external appearance or psychological mindset. It was inevitable that this similarity in the marketplace would be paralleled by a growing social consensus in virtually every other facet of the founding families' existence.

The founding families were much transformed by the evolution of structure in the society. Their adaptation to the increasingly elaborate systems was facilitated by the accumulation of advantages. Although inheritances of estates continued to be the most graphic and outstanding example of its functioning, the character of the other advantages inherent in being a founding family member changed drastically.

The children (and in some cases, grandchildren) of the family founders still lived in an age of face-to-face business contacts. For them the accumulation of advantages operated through a locally respected family reputation and a business network of family and friends. Its economic effectiveness depended upon business enterprises that could be controlled by a single person. In addition, all other social activities occurred within an equally individualized context. This permitted, and indeed mandated, the functioning of the accumulation of advantages within a social and technological milieu where memory and familiarity counted for more than factual listings in Dun and Bradstreet or the social register. Business and social relationships in 1820 did not depend on such systematized indicators and neither existed at the time.

As technological advances began to unite previously self-contained communities into a national network, it was no longer possible for the accumulation of advantages to depend upon local reputation and contacts to maintain the founding families in a position of economic and social dominance. The accumulation of advantages did not cease to function; however, it adapted to enlarged bureaucratized systems. Locally, family reputation continued to have much the same significance and influence as it did generations before. But nationally, the accumulation of advantages provided the means of obtaining all those indicators of position on which the upper class was becoming increasingly dependent. Church, school, and club, which had had little influence in determining social position on the local level in 1820, were vitally important at the national level by 1900. The accumulation of advantages had been transmuted into a universal and formalized system.

Founding family members who had migrated elsewhere were well served by the new systems. The distinctions which once so discernibly separated Allegheny County from the rest of the country had become blurred. Technology had largely overcome regional isolation and integrated the country into the larger social and economic fabric. Geography was no longer the limiting factor that it once was. This was reflected in migration of every type, but the direction of migration was now less important than the context in which it occurred, for it too was taking place within large-scale systems. These same large-scale systems, which were facilitating this new type of founding family migration, also facilitated the operation of the accumulation of advantages far beyond the county boundaries.

The same technology that was building a uniform national structure was also creating national markets and therefore national competition. The comparative advantages enjoyed by founding family business enterprises in a local market were gradually eroded after the Civil War. Technology was indeed a sword that could cut both ways. It may have aided a nationwide operation of the accumulation of advantages, but it also brought more highly competitive forces to bear on locally based businesses. Since technology was universally available, old founding family businesses were often hard-pressed to keep up. Local advantage provided only limited protection in terms of propinquity to markets or the loyalty of long-standing customers, for their competitors were often larger and more efficient—the very epitome of large-scale systems. When the family firms could no longer keep up with the corporate giants, they often sold out to them. Although founding family members bargained to assume executive positions in the larger company, they were almost never able to pass on these positions to their children. For many the security afforded by inheriting a position in a family firm had been the greatest advantage of being a founding family member. As this security slowly evaporated, they were compelled to use their advantages in other ways. While careers in business were still important—more frequently as executives in corporations instead of in family firms—they relied more heavily on the professions to provide the secure incomes necessary to maintain themselves within the elite upper class.

By the late nineteenth century the professions were undergoing a structural transformation similar to that affecting business. The informal methods of training used in the past were being replaced by formalized instruction at accredited institutions of higher learning. In the 1820s, in preparing a son for a career in law, for example, a founding family would employ the accumulation of advantages by having him read law under the direction of a locally prominent attorney. By 1900 a successful career in law began at a prestigious university. The founding families were able to finance the long and costly educational preparation that was a prerequisite for a truly eminent career. The old method depended upon familiarity, smallness of scale, and on the fame of the individual attorney; the new method relied on the reputation of an entire school. In their utilization of system and structure, the founding families drew upon the accumulation of advantages in a new way and gave their sons a comparative advantage over others.

The accumulation of advantages did not benefit the sons exclusively, however. All the founding families included daughters in the inheritance, usually in equal shares with sons. Although normally daughters did not receive the advantage of participation in the family firm or an education at a prestigious university, they benefited from the family reputation in selecting compatible and successful marriage partners. Their marriages were extremely stable and economically successful, often to professionals of considerable renown or successful businessmen whose wealth exceeded that of their own family. Their lives were usually spent in comfortable surroundings, free from the necessity of having to earn a living. Those who were well educated often pursued professional but nonremunerative occupations, but generally founding family daughters concerned themselves with society affairs, volunteer work, and the overseeing of their children's upbringing. Unmarried daughters, while not so fortunate in economic circumstances, dependent as they were on the family to maintain them, did receive the advantage of a place in society commensurate with their parents' positions.

Sons of the founding families were also able to marry well, utilizing the accumulation of advantages in terms of reputation, wealth, and social standing to win acceptance into equally notable families. Many of the family founders advanced themselves by marrying into wealthy and prestigious families. In many cases, their descendants were able to contract marriages with other local families of considerable fortune and connections. The advantage provided by marriage into a good family with its own network of personal and business associations advanced their careers, although few actually obtained positions in the family firm of the wife's family. As the context of founding family social interaction expanded from a local elite into a national upper class, the accumulation of advantages was employed in finding suitable mates from the larger pool of eligible daughters of the upper class through such connections as college and organization memberships. The marriages of founding family sons proved to be as stable as those of their sisters.

The ability of the founding families to adapt the accumulation of advantages to the changing character of the larger society's organizational structure resulted in a remarkable stability in the percentage of successful members in each generation. The fact that they were able to employ the accumulation of advantages despite changing economic and social circumstances might be interpreted by some as evidence of a closed American society. Since all the founding family names remained prominent, one could question whether nineteenth-century American society was characterized by any substantial degree of downward social mobility from the upper class. Yet about a fourth of the founding family members in each generation did decline and the others had to "hurry" in order to keep up. Even though there was room at the top, the competition was intense; every American was an incipient capitalist looking for the main chance. The number of positions within the elite upper class itself was limited to some extent, and there was a possibility that the dependents of the family founder could be displaced. They reaped the benefit of the family founders having been there "first," thus providing them with a head start, but this did not prove to be an infallible safeguard. For those who were successful, despite the accumulation of advantages from preceding generations, success was not guaranteed. Unlike the closed European model of society discussed in chapter 1, in which succeeding generations were seen as entrenched in inherited positions of power, sons of the founding families still had to vigorously pursue careers in order to maintain themselves. And as enormous post–Civil War fortunes were built in Allegheny County by comparative newcomers to the area, the founding families found themselves further separated from the pinnacle of wealth and power than their family founders had been.

Penetration from below into the upper class by new elites undeniably existed. Decline from the elite upper class to marginal or unsuccessful status also existed. To what extent, if any, the old elite had actually been displaced by the new may never be known. Indeed, upward and downward mobility were two independent variables and the term *displacement* may have no application. In an age of rapid technological development, opportunities seemed practically limitless. Therefore, one man's success did not necessarily require another man's failure. Such opportunities along with the population growth created a climate conducive to a relatively open society. Thus some sons of the marginal or unsuccessful founding family members were able to begin again the climb to the ranks of the successful.

The social structure was not entirely open, however. The self-made man did not have a chance of success equal to his privileged competitors. The race was decidedly handicapped in favor of the descendants of the successful who could employ the accumulation of advantages to launch themselves into successful careers. Even those sons of the marginal or unsuccessful, who regained elite positions, availed themselves of whatever remained of the accumulation of advantages. The founding families of Allegheny County were extremely successful in launching their young from advantageous positions. They carefully built their reputations and social positions, created ideal residential environments, contracted stable and economically secure marriages, limited the number of their children so as not to dilute inheritances, purchased the necessary educations, belonged to the proper organizations, and patterned their lives to conform with the standards of their class. In so doing, they endowed their young with as many prerequisites to success as they could possibly muster, adapting to their changing times, and giving their children a much-needed edge as they set off to challenge the future and remain elite upper class.

Appendix
Notes
Bibliography of Biographical Sources
Index

APPENDIX
The Founding Families

The following tables give a statistical overview of the founding families of Allegheny County. With the exception of the adjusted percentages, the figures are calculated for the entire sample of 1,006 individuals.

TABLE A
Family Size

Family Name	Number in Family	% of Total Sample
Anshutz	18	1.8
Bakewell	78	7.8
Brunot	17	1.7
Denny	68	6.8
Dilworth	59	5.9
Fahnestock	54	5.4
Gilfillan	29	2.9
Guthrie	59	5.9
Herron	60	6.0
Johnston	14	1.4
Liggett	25	2.5
McClure	82	8.2
Negley	157	15.6
Neville	38	3.8
Nimick	18	1.8
Ormsby	28	2.8
Page	55	5.5
Phillips	28	2.8
Sturgeon	97	9.6
Wrenshall	22	2.2

TABLE B
Core and Non-Core

	Number	Percent
Core	468	46.5
Non-Core	538	53.5

TABLE C
Males and Unmarried Females

	Number	Percent	Adjusted Percent
Male	935	92.9	93.3
Female	67	6.7	6.7
No information	4	0.4	—

TABLE D
Number and Percentage in Each Generation

Generation	Number	Percent	Adjusted Percent
1st	30	3.0	3.0
2nd	141	14.0	14.1
3rd	341	33.9	34.1
4th	412	41.0	41.2
5th	69	6.9	6.9
6th	7	0.7	0.7
Unassigned	6	0.6	—

TABLE E
Number and Percentage in Each Period

	Number	Percent	Adjusted Percent
1820	157	15.6	16.5
1860	368	36.6	38.8
1900	424	42.1	44.7
Unassigned	57	5.7	—

TABLE F
Place of Birth

	Number	Percent	Adjusted Percent
Pittsburgh	301	29.9	41.0
Allegheny County	137	13.6	18.6
Pennsylvania	110	10.9	15.0
Northeast	30	3.0	4.1
South	50	5.0	6.8
Midwest	56	5.6	7.6
West	2	0.2	0.3
Foreign	49	4.9	6.7
Unknown	271	26.9	—

TABLE G
Place of Death

	Number	Percent	Adjusted Percent
Pittsburgh	282	28.0	40.9
Allegheny County	98	9.7	14.2
Pennsylvania	88	8.7	12.8
Northeast	31	3.1	4.5
South	69	6.9	10.0
Midwest	83	8.3	12.0
West	29	2.9	4.2
Foreign	9	0.9	1.3
Unknown	317	31.5	—

TABLE H
Ethnicity

	Number	Percent	Adjusted Percent
English	266	26.4	34.2
Scotch-Irish	269	26.7	34.6
Scottish	69	6.9	8.9
Welsh	4	0.4	0.5
Irish	5	0.5	0.6
German	136	13.5	17.5
French	25	2.5	3.2
Scandinavian	1	0.1	0.1
Other	2	0.2	0.3
Unknown	229	22.8	—

TABLE I
Occupation: 1st through 6th

	1st	2nd	3rd	4th	5th	6th
Professional						
Judge	1	5	3	2	1	—
Lawyer	62	3	—	1	—	—
Doctor	35	2	—	2	—	—
Clergyman	32	1	—	—	—	—
Editor/author	6	11	9	3	3	—
Teacher	17	9	1	—	—	—
Engineer	29	2	3	—	—	—
Scientist	—	2	—	1	—	—
Commercial						
Banker	23	12	15	9	9	1
Merchant	30	11	1	1	—	—
Commission merchant	4	6	—	—	—	1
Shipper/wholesaler	18	14	5	2	2	2
Dry goods merchant	2	1	—	—	—	—
Broker	11	5	3	1	—	—
Real estate/insurance dealer	15	10	12	6	5	3
Agent/manager	18	14	6	2	—	—
Storeowner	14	9	3	1	1	1
Druggist	3	3	—	—	—	—
Hotel owner	4	—	—	—	—	—
Secretary/treasurer	4	14	9	6	1	—
President	2	13	10	5	4	3
Production (entrepreneurial)						
Manufacturer	12	13	4	6	1	1
Iron manufacturer	26	11	10	3	2	—
Glass manufacturer	4	4	2	3	—	—
Food product processor	11	17	7	1	2	1
Printer	7	4	—	—	—	—
Builder/contractor	5	3	5	1	2	—
Mine operator	4	7	6	2	—	—
Refinery owner/operator	5	4	3	2	2	—
Clerical/Mechanical						
Bookkeeper	6	4	1	—	1	1
Clerk	41	4	1	1	—	—
Mechanic	23	1	—	1	—	—
Laborer	4	—	—	—	—	—
Foreman	1	—	—	—	—	—

	1st	2nd	3rd	4th	5th	6th
Farming/Landholding						
Farmer	69	3	2	1	1	—
Landowner	9	24	9	3	—	2
Government						
Senator	—	—	1	—	—	—
Federal/state official	5	12	22	3	1	1
Local official (executive)	—	14	4	3	6	5
Local official	1	7	6	4	2	—
Military						
General	1	3	2	1	—	—
Colonel	7	1	2	5	1	1
Major	10	8	4	6	2	—
Captain	19	7	8	1	—	—
1st Lietuenant	7	8	2	—	—	—
2nd Lieutenant	15	2	—	—	—	—
Sergeant	2	1	—	—	—	—
Private	6	5	—	—	—	—
Miscellaneous						
Not employed	21	1	—	—	—	—
Philanthropist, patron of the arts, etc.	6	3	1	1	—	—
Unknown and/or none	349	688	835	916	957	983

Note: Reading across, the table shows that one person was a judge as his first occupation; five were judges as their second occupation; three were judges as their third occupation; and so forth.

TABLE J
Greatest Number of Jobs Held at One Time

Number of Jobs	Number of Persons	Percent	Adjusted Percent
1	338	33.6	74.3
2	74	7.4	16.3
3	27	2.7	5.9
4	7	0.7	1.5
5	5	0.5	1.1
6	3	0.3	0.7
7	1	0.1	0.2
0	551	54.8	—

TABLE K
Family Firm Employment

	Number	Percent	Adjusted Percent
Never in the family firm	174	17.3	50.1
Outside employment—family firm	19	1.9	5.5
Outside employment—family firm—outside employment	8	0.8	2.3
Family firm—outside employment	27	2.7	7.8
Family firm plus outside interests	43	4.3	12.4
Family firm only	76	7.6	21.9
Unknown	659	65.5	—

TABLE L
Occupations of Non-core Fathers

	Number	Percent	Adjusted Percent
Professional			
Judge	6	0.6	2.9
Lawyer	10	1.0	4.8
Doctor	14	1.4	6.8
Clergyman	18	1.8	8.7

	Number	Percent	Adjusted Percent
Editor/author	1	0.1	0.5
Engineer	4	0.4	1.9
Scientist	1	0.1	0.5
Commercial			
Banker	8	0.8	3.9
Merchant	10	1.0	4.8
Commission merchant	1	0.1	0.5
Shipper/wholesaler	1	0.1	0.5
Dry goods merchant	1	0.1	0.5
Broker	1	0.1	0.5
Agent/manager	2	0.2	1.0
Store owner	3	0.3	1.4
Hotel owner	2	0.2	1.0
Secretary	1	0.1	0.5
President	2	0.2	1.0
Production (entrepreneurial)			
Manufacturer	3	0.3	1.4
Iron manufacturer	13	1.3	6.3
Glass manufacturer	7	0.7	3.4
Food product processor	4	0.4	1.9
Builder/contractor	3	0.3	1.4
Mine owner/operator	1	0.1	0.5
Refinery owner/operator	1	0.1	0.5
Clerical/Mechanical			
Bookkeeper	1	0.1	0.5
Mechanic	2	0.2	1.0
Farming/Landholding			
Farmer	32	3.2	15.5
Landowner	17	1.7	8.2
Government			
Federal/state official	5	0.5	2.4
Local official	4	0.4	1.9
Military			
General	6	0.6	2.9
Colonel	9	0.9	4.3
Major	8	0.8	3.9
Captain	4	0.4	1.9
Private	1	0.1	0.5
Unknown	799	79.4	—

TABLE M
Residence

	1800	1810	1820	1830	1840	1850	1860	1870	1880	1890	1900	1910
Downtown/Hill	37	51	73	75	91	113	93	46	12	5	2	1
Allegheny City	3	2	2	2	6	22	33	39	35	34	31	8
South Side	4	7	7	7	10	20	15	5	2	1	2	1
Oakland/Hazlewood				1	1	1	6	5	9	16	17	10
East End	5	5	8	15	17	19	24	27	41	65	75	44
Allegheny County	30	38	49	61	77	83	76	66	55	39	41	27
Western Pennsylvania	10	16	23	22	24	33	46	55	50	43	26	14
East of Allegheny Mountains	23	16	21	18	14	17	19	25	26	23	18	14
South	5	13	22	28	24	25	19	15	16	11	14	10
West/Midwest	1	2	12	22	33	45	53	47	50	54	39	26
Foreign	8	5	6	8	1	6	8	7	5	3	2	3
Unknown	5	15	24	41	57	73	108	160	147	87	37	14

TABLE N
Place of Marriage

	Number	Percent	Adjusted Percent
Pittsburgh	202	20.1	48.2
Allegheny County	76	7.6	18.1
Pennsylvania	52	5.2	12.4
Northeast	19	1.9	4.5
South	16	1.6	3.8
Midwest	37	3.7	8.8
West	4	0.4	1.0
Foreign	13	1.3	3.1
Unknown	587	58.3	—

TABLE O
Married a Relative?

	Number	Percent	Adjusted Percent
Yes	20	2.0	2.5
No	767	76.2	97.5
Unknown	219	21.8	—

TABLE P
Number of Children

Number of Children in Family	Number of Families	Percent	Adjusted Percent
1	98	9.7	15.7
2	124	12.3	19.9
3	118	11.7	18.9
4	85	8.4	13.6
5	66	6.6	10.6
6	49	4.9	7.9
7	31	3.1	5.0
8	27	2.7	4.3
9	13	1.3	2.1
10	8	0.8	1.3
11	3	0.3	0.5
12	1	0.1	0.2
14	1	0.1	0.2
Unknown or 0	382	38.0	—

TABLE Q
Religion

	Number	Percent	Adjusted Percent
Episcopalian	71	7.1	21.8
Presbyterian	198	19.7	60.9
Presbyterian Sects	2	0.2	0.6
Methodist	24	2.4	7.4
German Reformed	4	0.4	1.2
Lutheran	7	0.7	2.2
Baptist	4	0.4	1.2
Roman Catholic	10	1.0	3.1
Other	5	0.5	1.5
Unknown	681	67.7	—

TABLE R
Education

Level/Location	Number	Percent	Adjusted Percent
Negligible	39	3.9	11.3
Grade School	37	3.7	10.8
High School	23	2.3	6.7
College (unspecified)	51	5.1	14.8
Western University of Pennsylvania (University of Pittsburgh)	32	3.2	9.3
Pittsburgh (other)	17	1.7	4.9
Washington and Jefferson (includes antecedents)	20	2.0	5.8
Tri-state area (Western Pa, Northern W.Va., Eastern Ohio)	6	0.6	1.7
Pennsylvania (not University of Pennsylvania)	17	1.7	4.9
Harvard	3	0.3	0.9
Princeton	20	2.0	5.8
Yale	11	1.1	3.2
Other Ivy League	15	1.5	4.4
Other Colleges by Region			
East	27	2.7	7.8
South	6	0.6	1.7
West/Midwest	10	1.0	2.9
Foreign	10	1.0	2.9
Unknown	662	65.8	—

NOTES

PREFACE

1. Frank L. Owsley, *Plain Folk of the Old South* (Baton Rouge: Louisiana State University Press, 1949; rpt. Chicago: Quadrangle Paperbacks, 1965), p. 153.

CHAPTER I
The Historical Framework

1. *Main chance* is used in a twentieth-century context by William E. Leuchtenberg: "like a Main Street banker with his eye on the main chance" (*Franklin Roosevelt and the New Deal* [New York: Harper & Row, 1963], p. 59); and by Douglas Dowd in a nineteenth-century context with the same meaning: "And when settled, the West was thinly settled, by people whose eyes were fixed on the main chance" ("A Comparative Analysis of Economic Development in the American West and South," *Journal of Economic History* 16 [1956]: 563. The term *takeoff*, made famous by Walter W. Rostow, *Stages of Economic Growth: A Non-Communist Manifesto* (New York: Cambridge University Press, 1960), is more commonly applied to economic systems; but *break*, with a similar meaning, almost always refers to individuals and is the most common of the three expressions both inside and outside academic circles. Its widespread use can be interpreted as a measure of belief among Americans that such a phenomenon does in fact exist. "All Americans—including workers—were incipient capitalists waiting for 'the break' " (Carl Degler, *Out of Our Past: The Forces That Shaped Modern America* [New York: Harper & Row, 1959], p. 263).

2. C. Wright Mills, *Power, Politics, and People; the Collected Essays of C. Wright Mills* (New York: Oxford University Press, 1963), p. 316.

3. A host of books and articles has been written about social stratification and power. Most of them deal, in part at least, with "the accumulation of advantages," even if only to deny its existence.

The difficulties encountered when dealing with the phenomenon of power were outlined in "An Analysis of Social Power" by Robert Bierstedt (*American Sociological Review* 15 [Dec. 1950]: 730–38), which warned of the dangers in trying to draw relationships among power, status, and prestige, calling them "independent variables," but admitting that they frequently occur together.

While the operation of the accumulation of advantages is the exercise of power, it need not take the same form. Power is latent force producing involuntary compliance. The accumulation of advantages can assume this form, but it more often may involve use of status and/or prestige, inducing voluntary compliance not through coercion but through influence. James A. Henretta gives an example: "The best opportunities for advancement rested with those who could draw upon long-standing connections, upon credit facilities of friends and neighbors, and upon political influence. It was precisely these personal contacts which were denied to the propertyless" ("Economic Development and Social Structure in Colonial Boston," *William and Mary Quarterly*, 3d ser., 22 [Jan. 1965]: 75–92). Under these circumstances, in which the accumulation of advantages is effectively demonstrated, coercion based upon power would have had less effect than influence based upon status and/or prestige.

Disagreeing with the concept of the accumulation of advantages, Kingsley Davis sees two factors as major determinants of the magnitude of the rewards attached to one's position in society: one's functional importance for that society and the relative scarcity of qualified personnel. One can only wonder how the individual obtained the position or qualifications in the first place. See *Human Society* (New York: Macmillan, 1949).

Using a less narrow definition, Gerhard E. Lenski summarizes his position: "The rewards which men and positions enjoy are a function of the degree to which their qualities, performances, and possessions measure up to the standards set by their society." While this is broad enough to include the accumulation of advantages, Lenski insists that his "underlying theoretical orientation is functionalist" (*Power and Privilege: A Theory of Social Stratification* [New York: McGraw-Hill, 1966], p. 16. See also: Suzanne I. Keller, *Beyond the Ruling Class: Strategic Elites in Societies* (New York: Random House, 1970); Floyd Hunter, *Community Power Structure: A Study of Decision Makers* (Chapel Hill: University of North Carolina Press, 1953); Barrington Moore, *Political Power and Social Theory* (Cambridge, Mass.: Harvard University Press, 1958), pp. 1–29; Morris Janowitz,

Community Political Systems (Glencoe, Ill.: Free Press, 1961); and Edward O. Laumann, *Prestige and Association in an Urban Community* (Indianapolis: Bobbs-Merrill, 1966).

4. Researchers have generally avoided discussion concerning the validity of inferring social mobility from occupational mobility. The possible reasons for this are explained by Charles F. Westoff, Marvin Bressler, and Philip C. Sagi in "The Concept of Social Mobility: An Empirical Inquiry," *American Sociological Review* 25 (June 1960): 378: "This practice has arisen partly as a concession to methodological difficulties and partly from theoretical considerations supported by empirical evidence."

I do not imply that occupation is not the single most important indicator of status and mobility. Seymour Martin Lipset and Reinhard Bendix, who incidentally do examine downward mobility, do not share these authors' concern. Relying on William Lloyd Warner's *Social Class in America* (Chicago: Science Research Associates, 1949), they insist that "the major effort to construct a scale of social-status positions in America employs occupational position as one of the principal items in the scale" (*Social Mobility in Industrial Society* [Berkeley and Los Angeles: University of California Press, 1959], p. 156). For a bibliography of mobility studies see R. W. Mack, L. Freeman, and S. Yellin, *Social Mobility: Thirty Years of Research and Theory* (Syracuse: Syracuse University Press, 1957).

5. The pioneering quantitative work which attempts to measure the openness of American society in the nineteenth century is Stephen Thernstrom, *Poverty and Progress: Social Mobility in a Nineteenth-Century City* (New York: Atheneum, 1969). His time period of thirty years is too short to detect any change in the rate of mobility, though intergenerational social mobility is central to the theme. While he uses the same broad occupational categories as Lipset in determining social mobility, it is supplemented by data on property and savings.

6. Edward Digby Baltzell, *Philadelphia Gentlemen: The Making of a National Upper Class* (New York: Free Press, 1958). Aside from a table (pp. 71–77) listing individuals and their accomplishments, and selected biographies, he does not develop this theme.

7. The table "Proper Philadelphia Families: Elite Members, 1682–1940" lists 66 families and 172 persons, only 2.6 notable persons per family. Baltzell, *Philadelphia Gentlemen*, p. 71.

8. It is conceivable that there are individuals born in Philadelphia who, in 1940, lived elsewhere, are listed in *Who's Who in America*, and continue to be listed in Philadelphia's *Social Register*. Because

they did not reside in Philadelphia in 1940, they are excluded from Baltzell's group. At the same time Baltzell points out as a weakness of the "Warner School" that "they fail to make explicit that horizontal and vertical mobility are usually rather closely associated variables." *Pihladelphia Gentlemen*, p. 159.

9. Stuart Mack Blumin, "Mobility in a Nineteenth-Century American City: Philadelphia, 1820–1860" (Ph.D. diss., University of Pennsylvania, 1968), p. 12.

10. Edward Pessen, *Riches, Class, and Power Before the Civil War* (Lexington, Mass: D. C. Heath & Co., 1973).

11. Lee Benson, "Philadelphia Elites and Economic Development: Quasi-Public Innovation During the First American Organizational Revolution," *Working Papers of the Eleutherian Mills–Hagley Foundation* (1978).

12. Frederick Cople Jaher, *The Urban Establishment: Upper Strata in Boston, New York, Charleston, Chicago, and Los Angeles* (Urbana: University of Illinois Press, 1982).

13. William Miller, "American Historians and the Business Elite," *Journal of Economic History* 9 (Nov. 1949).

14. John N. Ingham, *The Iron Barons: A Social Analysis of an American Urban Elite, 1874–1965* (Westport, Conn.: Greenwood Press, 1978).

15. Burton W. Folsom, Jr., *Urban Capitalists: Entrepreneurs and City Growth in Pennsylvania's Lackawanna and Lehigh Region, 1800–1920* (Baltimore: The Johns Hopkins University Press, 1981).

CHAPTER II
Discovering the Founding Families

1. For a discussion of the terms *elite* and *upper class*, see the beginning of Chapter 5.

2. Frank W. Powelson, "Founding Families of Allegheny County, 5 vols. (Pittsburgh, 1963), vol. 1, p. 1. The original manuscript is located in the Pennsylvania Division, Carnegie Library of Pittsburgh, Pittsburgh, Pennsylvania. Cited below as "Powelson's index" or "Powelson's 'Founding Families.' "

3. Among the lists that Powelson used was *A Chronological Table of the Judges and Other Officers of Allegheny County*, together with an alphabetical list of the members of the bar since the formation of the county by Daniel W. Olegar (Pittsburgh, 1863). He also used a num-

ber of local and regional encyclopedias, some of which are attributed in his manuscript such as Frank C. Harper, *Pittsburgh of Today: Its Resources and People*, 5 vols. (New York: The American Historical Society, 1931).

Powelson frequently gives Masonic Lodge affiliation in his genealogies. The Masons were undeniably the most prestigious social organization in the county in the late seventeenth and early eighteenth centuries. However, masonic membership and lodge affiliation are significant to my own study only in the identification of the first generation elite and are not traced in later generations. The Masons are discussed in greater detail in chapters 4 and 7.

4. John Taylor and R. Patterson, "Prominent Citizens of Pittsburgh, Pennsylvania," *Honest Man's Almanac* (Pittsburgh: Patterson and Hopkins, 1812). A directory of Pittsburgh and its vicinity for 1812–13, published by Patterson and Hopkins, booksellers, it includes business or profession and city address.

5. Where it seemed logical to include those born after 1880 (e.g., a family's last child), I did so.

6. John Newton Boucher, ed., *A Century and a Half of Pittsburgh and Her People*, 4 vols. (New York: The Lewis Historical Publishing Co., 1908), vol. 3, p. 46.

7. *The Biographical Encyclopedia of Pennsylvania of the Nineteenth Century* (Philadelphia: Galaxy Publishing Co., 1874), p. 640; George Thornton Fleming, *History of Pittsburgh and Environs*, 6 vols. (New York: The American Historical Society, 1922), vol. 4, p. 62; Allen Johnson, *Dictionary of American Biography*, 20 vols. (New York: Charles Scribner's Sons, 1929), vol. 13, p. 405.

8. John W. Jordan, *Encyclopedia of Pennsylvania Biography*, 32 vols. (New York: The Lewis Historical Publishing Co., 1914), vol. 11, pp. 282–83.

9. *Pittsburgh and Pennsylvania Genealogies (Fragmenta Genealogica Heraldica)* (Pittsburgh: Pierpont, Siviter & Co., 1906), vol. 1, pp. 5–8.

10. Boucher, *Century and a Half*, vol. 3, p. 46. The "other source" is George Thornton Fleming, *History of Pittsburgh and Environs*, 6 vols. (New York: American Historical Society, 1922), vol. 4, p. 102.

11. William Alfred Herron and William Herron Hezlep, "Our Herron Family of Allegheny County, Pennsylvania" (Pittsburgh, 1960, mimeographed), p. 15.

12. For a discussion of the levels of statistical significance and chi square, see William Buchanan, *Understanding Political Variables* (New York: Charles Scribner's Sons, 1969), pp. 80–99, 114–25.

CHAPTER III
The Family Founders

1. Russell J. Ferguson, *Early Western Pennsylvania Politics* (Pittsburgh: University of Pittsburgh Press, 1938), p. 2.

2. Ibid., p. 2.

3. Ibid., p. 4.

4. *Encyclopedia of Pennsylvania Biography*, vol. 31, pp. 25–28. Additional information on the Ormsbys from: Oliver Ormsby Page, *Short Account of the Family of Ormsby* (Albany, N.Y.: Munsell, 1892), and Robert McKnight, "Diaries: 1840–1842," Darlington Memorial Library, University of Pittsburgh.

5. John W. Jordan, *Colonial and Revolutionary Families of Pennsylvania,* 17 vols. (New York: Lewis Publishing Co., 1911), vol. 2, pp. 955–57.

6. John Neville was the only family founder to have a land grant from Virginia since both Pennsylvania and Virginia claimed the land as part of their territory. Pennsylvania had relatively few large landholdings owing to the land policies followed by the colony's proprietors, but Virginian estates were far more extensive. Neville, true to the Virginia upper-class tradition of western landholding, held as much as ten thousand acres of land in his life.

7. Information on John McClure is from Cicero Pangburn McClure and Roy Fleming McClure, *Pioneer McClure Families of the Monongahela Valley: Their Origins and Their Descendants* (Akron, Ohio: Superior Printing Co., 1924).

8. The conflicting land claims of Virginia and Pennsylvania posed certain problems. In 1775, two years after John Ormsby was granted a Pennsylvania license to operate a ferry service across the Monongahela river, a Virginia court granted a similar license to someone else at the same location (Leland D. Baldwin, *Pittsburgh: The Story of a City* [Pittsburgh: University of Pittsburgh Press, 1937], p. 101; Solon J. Buck and Elizabeth H. Buck, *The Planting of Civilization in Western Pennsylvania* [Pittsburgh: University of Pittsburgh Press, 1939], pp. 238, 239). Margaret Gilfillan related how family founder Alexander Gilfillan marked the trees to his claim. The practice was to apply for the land to the surveyor general's office of either Pennsylvania or Virginia, depending upon which state the applicant thought had jurisdiction. Alexander applied to the Pennsylvania state capital on February 10, 1785 (Margaret Gilfillan, *Alexander Gilfillan, 1746–1836; Martha Gilfillan, 1759–1840* [Pittsburgh, 1955], pp. 10–11).

9. Leland D. Baldwin, *Whiskey Rebels: The Story of a Frontier Uprising* (Pittsburgh: University of Pittsburgh Press, 1939), and H. M. Brackenridge, *History of the Western Insurrection, Called the Whiskey Insurrection, 1794* (Pittsburgh: W. S. Haven, 1859).

10. Felix C. Negley, *Traditional History and Family Record of the Negley Family* (Pittsburgh: H. L. McGraw and Son, 1898).

11. Margaret Collins Denny Dixon and Elizabeth Denny Vann, *Denny Genealogy* (New York: National Historical Society, 1944).

12. John Johnston, the sole manufacturer among the self-made family founders, spent much of his career accumulating the capital necessary to build his wire works. William G. Johnston, *Life and Reminiscences from Birth to Manhood of William G. Johnston* (New York: Knickerbocker Press, 1901).

13. Buck, *The Planting of Civilization*, pp. 152–55. To determine the ethnic composition of Western Pennsylvania, the Bucks used the method of distinctive surnames as developed by Howard F. Barker in the *American Historical Association Annual Report, 1931* (Washington, D.C., 1932), pp. 126–359. The breakdown for Allegheny County in 1790 was: English, 43 percent; Welsh, 8 percent; Scottish, 25 percent; Irish, 16 percent; German, 4 percent; other, 4 percent. Irish includes Scotch-Irish, English-Irish, and Ulster Celts, all of whom were Protestant, and Catholic South Irish. The remaining 6 percent were Catholic–South Irish. It is probable that a large proportion of the Scottish percentage, perhaps two-thirds, was actually Scotch-Irish. If the Scottish and Irish are considered as Scotch-Irish, the combination of the two results in a percentage approaching that of the English by 1790. If the founding families' ethnic breakdown and the number of Scotch-Irish Presbyterian churches are accepted as indicators, then the Scotch-Irish achieved numerical superiority over the English by 1820.

14. William E. Liggett, "Biographical Sketches of the Foulks-Liggett Families" (University City, Mo., 1957, mimeographed).

15. Benjamin Gifford Bakewell, *The Family Book of Bakewell, Page and Campbell* (Pittsburgh: William G. Johnston and Co., 1896). Additional information on Page family descendants from: Anne Hollingsworth Wharton, *Genealogy of the Wharton Family of Philadelphia, 1664–1880* (Philadelphia: Privately printed, 1880).

16. Harold M. Pitman, *The Fahnestock Genealogy: Ancestors and Descendants of Johann Diedrich Fahnestock* (Concord, N.H.: Rumford Press, ca. 1945).

17. John Wrenshall, "Autobiography," vol. 3, a manuscript cited

by Jacob Simpson Payton, *Our Fathers Have Told Us: The Story of the Founding of Methodism in Western Pennsylvania* (Cincinnati: Ruter Press, 1938), pp. 120–27.

18. Virginia W. Bushman, "Dilworth Families in America" (Philadelphia, n.d., photoduplicated, original in the Historical Society of Pennsylvania).

CHAPTER IV
The Founding Families in 1820

1. The U.S. population grew by 25 percent from 1810 to 1820; Pennsylvania experienced a 23 percent increase.

2. U.S. Census Office, *Third Census* (1810); *Fourth Census* (1820); *Fifth Census* (1830).

3. *Pittsburgh Gazette*, August 17, 1830.

4. Although exact year of birth is unknown for many non-core husbands, their inclusion in this group can be assumed from the known age of their wives, the daughters of the founding families. Place of birth for the non-core husbands was more frequently recorded, especially if outside the United States.

5. U.S. Census, 1820, and Sarah H. Killikelly, *The History of Pittsburgh: Its Rise and Progress* (Pittsburgh: B. C. Gordon Montgomery Co., 1906), p. 166.

6. James M. Riddle, *The Pittsburgh Directory for 1815* (Pittsburgh, 1815).

7. Catherine E. Reiser, *Pittsburgh's Commercial Development, 1800–1850* (Harrisburg: Pennsylvania Historical and Museum Commission, 1951), p. 2.

8. On the early development of the Ohio River towns, 1790–1830, see Richard C. Wade, *The Urban Frontier: Pioneer Life in Early Pittsburgh, Cincinnati, Lexington, Louisville, and St. Louis* (Chicago: University of Chicago Press, 1959).

9. Though theories concerning subsistence farming on the frontier have been challenged, it is clear that rural Allegheny County could not be considered as a cash-based economy even in 1820 when it was long past the so-called frontier stage of development.

10. Proof of this can be found in the tax assessment records of Allegheny Pennsylvania, *City Records 1824–1907*, in the Archives of Industrial Society at the University of Pittsburgh. A tax was levied on each occupation presumably in accordance with its value or income.

Some clerks were taxed three times the amount of others, a greater disparity than in almost all other occupations.

11. Sylvester K. Stevens and Donald H. Kent, eds., *County Government and Archives in Pennsylvania* (Harrisburg: Pennsylvania Historical and Museum Commission, 1947), pp. 1–13; *Pennsylvania Manual, 1970–1971* (Harrisburg: Department of Property and Supplies, 1971), p. 525; League of Women Voters, *Allegheny County Government: Organization, Facilities and Services* (Pittsburgh, 1971), p. 6.

12. Killikelly, *The History of Pittsburgh*, pp. 154–56.

13. *History of Allegheny County, Pennsylvania* (Chicago: A. Warner & Co., 1889), pp. 625–26.

14. *A Digest of the Acts of Assembly Relating to, and the General Ordinances of the City of Pittsburgh from 1804 to Nov. 12, 1908* (Pittsburgh: Market Review Publishing Co., 1909), pp. 949–51. For example, five of the first six mayors of Pittsburgh are in Powelson's index; one is in the founding family sample. Of the fourteen presidents of the Select Council, 1816–1851, nine are in Powelson's index and five are in the sample.

15. It was not until 1877 that a judge of the Court of Common Pleas was elevated to the state Supreme Court. During the period when the post was appointive, 1791–1850, six persons held it, two of whom are in Powelson's index.

16. Harriet N. Dunn and Evaline Dunn, *Records of the Guthrie Family of Pennsylvania, Connecticut and Virginia, with Ancestry of Those Who Have Intermarried with the Family* (Chicago: H. A. and S. I. Dunn, 1898). See also family histories cited in chapter 3.

17. Claudius T. McCoy, *A Genealogical History of the Sturgeons of North America* (Cincinnati, 1926).

18. Anne Newport Royall, "Pennsylvania," ca. 1828, reprinted in George Swetnam, *The Bicentennial History of Pittsburgh and Allegheny County* (Pittsburgh: Historical Record Association, 1955), vol. 1, pp. 43–44.

19. Solon J. Buck and Elizabeth M. Buck, *The Planting of Civilization in Western Pennsylvania* (Pittsburgh: University of Pittsburgh Press, 1939), p. 349.

20. Robert E. Harper, "The Class Structure of Western Pennsylvania in the Late Eighteenth Century" (Ph.D. diss., University of Pittsburgh, 1969), pp. 179–89. He divided the population into six, sometimes five, categories according to occupation: professional, mercantile (yeoman), artisan dependent or laboring, and speculator. In Connellsville in 1796, for instance, the median taxable

wealth for each occupation category was $1,058, $375, $600, $165, $45, and $80 respectively (p. 181). It should be noted that this inequality occurred in but a single generation, an era typically described as equalitarian—economically, socially, and politically.

21. Russell J. Ferguson, *Early Western Pennsylvania Politics* (Pittsburgh: University of Pittsburgh Press, 1938), p. 8.

22. Watson, "Annuals" dated 1743 as cited by Margaret Collins Denny Dixon and Elizabeth Denny Vann, *Denny Genealogy* (New York: National Historical Society, 1944), pp. 5–6. At first the Scotch-Irish had been well received. Penn's agent, Secretary James Logan, reported, "The Scotch-Irish if kindly used, will, I believe be orderly, as they have hitherto been and easily dealt with, they will also be a leading example to others." Shortly thereafter, however, he complained that they were "audacious and disorderly"; in 1730 he reported that "the settlement of five families from Ireland gives me more troubles than fifty of any other people" (p. 5).

23. Buck, *The Planting of Civilization*, pp. 140–43. They estimate the Scottish population for Allegheny County at 25 percent of the total. It is conceivable that a portion of this, perhaps most, belongs to the Scotch-Irish.

24. Killikelly, *The History of Pittsburgh*, pp. 139–40.

25. Taylor and Patterson, "Prominent Citizens of Pittsburgh, Pennsylvania." It gave the names of only 63 merchants, storekeepers, and innkeepers whereas the *Pittsburgh Directory for 1815* listed 202. The editors promised that the directory for 1814 "will be considerably enlarged." Interestingly, they did not forget to include themselves in the "first" edition.

Although the almanac listed only prominent urbanites, 31 percent are in Powelson's index, nine of whom are in the founding family sample. If the number seems small, it should be noted that of the twenty families, two had not yet arrived and six were rural. (Presley Neville, the sole surviving son was away in Harrisburg serving in state government and John Herron was still a clerk in a lumber business awaiting the main chance.)

26. Leland D. Baldwin, *Pittsburgh: The Story of a City* (Pittsburgh: University of Pennsylvania Press, 1937), p. 110. Charles W. Dahlinger concurs with Baldwin's assessment of the Masons. Describing them in 1810 he writes, "Practically all the leaders in the village, whether in public or private life, had been or were still members of the lodge" (*Pittsburgh: A Sketch of Its Early Social Life* [New York: G. P. Putnam's Sons, 1916], p. 95).

27. Dahlinger, *Pittsburgh*, pp. 12–13. Evidence of this alliance occurred on two occasions each year, St. John the Baptist's Day and St. John the Evangelist's Day, when the Masons marched in procession from the lodge house to the Presbyterian church where the minister preached a sermon.

28. Information on this and the following organizations was obtained from Riddle, *Pittsburgh Directory*, pp. 120–28.

29. Buck, *The Planting of Civilization*, p. 351.

30. A case for the existence of social stratification in Pittsburgh in 1815 can be made. The fire companies, with identical aims, represent a clear-cut chance for decision making on the part of both the prospective member and the organization itself. Both the Eagle and the Vigilant companies claimed sons of the city's most substantial families as members, but the Vigilant consisted mainly of craftsmen.

31. Dahlinger, *Pittsburgh*, pp. 93–94.

32. Ibid., p. 94.

33. Quoted by Jacob Simpson Payton, *Our Fathers Have Told Us: The Story of the Founding of Methodism in Western Pennsylvania* (Cincinnati: Ruter Press, 1938), vol. 3, pp. 29–39.

34. *Centennial Volume of the First Presbyterian Church of Pittsburgh, Pennsylvania, 1784–1884* (Pittsburgh, 1884), p. 28; Dahlinger, *Pittsburgh*, p. 84.

35. True class distinctions could not have existed in the Pittsburgh of 1820 given the limitations which population size and lack of sophistication of the social institutions imposed. But stratification is indigenous to any form of human association, and in the absence of a better word, *class* will have to suffice.

36. *The Pittsburgh Directory for 1815*, p. 130.

37. Buck, *The Planting of Civilization*, pp. 351–52.

38. Killikelly, *The History of Pittsburgh*, pp. 355–68.

39. Luther B. Reed, *The History of the First English Evangelical Lutheran Church in Pittsburgh, 1837–1909* (Philadelphia: J. B. Lippincott, 1909), p. 4.

40. Killikelly, *The History of Pittsburgh*, p. 379.

41. William L. Warner, *History of Allegheny County Pennsylvanians* (Chicago: A. Warner and Co., 1889), p. 267.

42. Dahlinger, *Pittsburgh*, pp. 95–96. He lists eight prominent citizens who were manufacturers of, or dealers in, intoxicating liquors in 1810. Six of them appeared in *The Pittsburgh Directory for 1815*, five years after Pittsburgh's first temperance reform, but only one reported dealing in liquor. Four were innkeepers (probably tav-

ernkeepers), one a grocer, and one a wine manufacturer. While most avoided reporting a direct connection with liquor, it does not necessarily follow that they actually abandoned that occupation, however. Two of the six were founding family members.

43. Killikelly, *The History of Pittsburgh*, pp. 125–26, 356–57, 364–65; *Pittsburgh Gazette*, March 1808.

44. Buck, *The Planting of Civilization*, p. 365.

45. Ibid.

46. Wade, *The Urban Frontier*, pp. 143–44. Buck, *The Planting of Civilization*, pp. 365–68. The Bucks make the distinction between professional theater which they claim "was not particularly successful in Pittsburgh or elsewhere in western Pennsylvania in the early days" (p. 365), and amateur theatricals which "appear to have had a certain vogue on the frontier" (p. 366).

47. He also was president of the Select Council, president of the Teacher's Lyceum of Allegheny County, president of the board of directors of the South Ward Public School, and president of the Pittsburgh Historical Society.

48. Killikelly, *The History of Pittsburgh*, p. 343.

CHAPTER V
Occupation

1. For the evolution of the elite into an upper class, see Dixon Wecter, *The Saga of American Society* (New York: Charles Scribner's Sons, 1937). For a discussion of the overlapping of the American elite and upper class, see Edward Digby Baltzell, *Philadelphia Gentlemen: The Making of a National Upper Class* (New York: Free Press, 1958), pp. 3–14.

2. The degree to which founding family females married within their own socioeconomic class will be discussed in detail in chapter 7.

3. Cleveland Amory, *The Proper Bostonians* (New York: E. P. Dutton, 1947), pp. 39–40.

4. Alfred D. Chandler, "The Beginnings of 'Big Business' in American Industry," *Business History Review* 33 (Spring 1959): 1–30.

5. Brooks Adams, *The Law of Civilization and Decay* (New York: Macmillan, 1896), p. vii.

6. John W. Jordan, *Colonial and Revolutionary Families of Pennsylvania*, 17 vols. (New York: The Lewis Historical Publishing Co., 1911), vol. 3, pp. 1547–51.

7. Jordan, *Encyclopedia of Pennsylvania Biography*, vol. 5, pp. 1635, 1637; Fleming, *History of Pittsburgh*, vol. 4, pp. 59, 61.

8. *History of Allegheny County Pennsylvanians*, vol. 2, p. 358.

9. *Biographical Review, Volume 24, Containing Life Sketches of Leading Citizens of Pittsburgh, Pennsylvania and the Vicinity* (Boston: Biographical Review Publishing Co., 1897), p. 13.

10. *The Manufactories and Manufacturing of Pennsylvania of the Nineteenth Century* (Philadelphia: Galaxy Publishing Co., 1875), p. 175.

11. Alexander P. Moore, *The Book of Prominent Pennsylvanians* (Pittsburgh: Leader Publishing Co., 1913), p. 155.

12. Benjamin Gifford Bakewell, *The Family Book of Bakewell, Page and Campbell* (Pittsburgh: William G. Johnston and Co., 1896), pp. 33–36; Jordan, *Encyclopedia of Pennsylvania Biography*, vol. 6, p. 2169.

13. William Henry Egle, *Pennsylvania: Genealogy Chiefly Scotch-Irish and German* (Baltimore: Genealogical Publishing Co., 1896); Warner, *History of Allegheny County*, vol. 1, pp. 87, 533, vol. 2, p. 216.

14. Harmer D. Denny spent his entire life "curating" the family inheritance, yet he was listed in Smith's *Notable Men* with the business designation of "real estate." This may be a reflection of the decision making required in the management of a landed estate as well as the popular work ethic. Percy F. Smith, *Notable Men of Pittsburgh and Vicinity* (Pittsburgh: Pittsburgh Printing Co., 1901), p. 341.

15. Jordan, *Colonial and Revolutionary Families*.

16. Frank C. Harper, *Pittsburgh of Today: Its Resources and People*, 5 vols. (New York: The American Historical Society, 1931), John Liggett, Jr.

17. Jackson Turner Main, *The Social Structure of Revolutionary America* (Princeton: Princeton University Press, 1965), pp. 200–01. Main concluded that "it seems probable that the general reputation of lawyers was higher than that of doctors" (p. 205). The largely unregulated medical profession was divided into physicians and pretenders; their income and status varied greatly. None of the founding family doctors were pretenders, although Dr. Bedford's biography says that he "read medicine;" no mention was made of formal education.

18. William H. Venable, *Beginnings of Literary Culture in the Ohio Valley* (Cincinnati: Robert Clarke and Co., 1891), pp. 373–75.

19. Harper, *Pittsburgh of Today*, vol. 5, p. 800.

20. Ibid.

21. Sources disagree on the status of the clergy. Jackson Turner Main reports that during the Revolutionary era the prestige of the clergy had declined to what he calls "an intermediate position on the

scale of prestige. . . . nevertheless they were still respected, and their influence was considerable" (*Social Structure*, pp. 206–07). A study of Hamilton, Ontario, in 1852 divided the occupations into four major divisions according to status. Clergymen did not rank in the first group but in the second highest group along with such occupations as tax collector, apothecary, and chairmaker (Michael B. Katz, "Occupation Classification in History," *Journal of Interdisciplinary History* 3 [Summer 1972]: 87).

22. The declining social status of the clergy did not necessarily cause fewer founding family members to choose it as a career. It may be argued that since the higher social strata (i.e., the founding families) were abandoning the ministry, their places were taken by those of plebian background, thus lowering the social status of the clergy.

23. This mobility is unique neither to the nineteenth century nor to the founding families. Witness these complaining words of a more recent time: "You take away his [the minister's] salary and he's nothin'! When he gets a chance to make more money at another place he calls it a call from God!" (Robert S. Lynd and Helen M. Lynd, *Middletown: A Study of American Culture* [New York: Harcourt, Brace & World, 1929], p. 348).

24. The military may not have enjoyed a high social status in 1900, but the same does not hold true for the founding period. The local upper class continued to be dominated by the military even after the dismantling of Fort Pitt in the 1790s as Fort Fayette, also in Pittsburgh, took its place. Solon and Elizabeth Buck's similar but less emphatic statement regarding its position has already been noted (Solon J. Buck and Elizabeth Buck, *The Planting of Civilization in Western Pennsylvania* [Pittsburgh: University of Pittsburgh Press, 1939], p. 349).

25. It should be noted, however, that of those born in the first period, 51 percent of the total, the percentage of those who were not successful was seven percentage points below the founding family average. Consequently the association between a military career and marginal success as expressed in Yule's Q measure of association is rather small.

	Number Declined	*Number Successful*
Military	12	31
Founding Family	139	427

$$\begin{array}{|c|c|} \hline a & b \\ \hline c & d \\ \hline \end{array} \; Q = \frac{ad - bc}{ad + bc} = \frac{12 \times 427 - 31 \times 139}{12 \times 427 + 31 \times 139}$$

$$= \frac{5124 - 4309}{5124 + 4309} = \frac{815}{9433} = +.086$$

As measured by Yule's Q, where +1.0 is perfect positive association, the association between a military career and marginal success is very small indeed.

26. While dependence of the military on other nonmilitary family members was the rule, it was not without exception. Edward Harding (1800–1855), husband of Nancy Denny, was commandant of the Mount Vernon Arsenal in Mobile, Alabama. Social life there was so lively that several cousins from Carlisle (Pennsylvania) came to visit and several stayed permanently.

27. Oliver Ormsby Page, *Short Account of the Family of Ormsby* (Albany, N.Y.: Munsell, 1892), p. 38.

28. Eight attended West Point; one attended Annapolis.

29. Employing Yule's Q once again reveals a quite strong association between core and leaving and non-core and staying.

	Core	Non-core
Left military	12	3
Stayed in Military	11	17
Q = +.7468		

30. John E. Parke, *Recollections of Seventy Years and Historical Gleanings of Allegheny, Pennsylvania* (Boston: Rand, Avery and Co., 1886), p. 35. Few founding family members joined it (Presley Neville was a sergeant in the War of 1812); they preferred another unit, the Duquesne Grays.

31. William G. Johnston, *Life and Reminiscences from Birth to Manhood of William G. Johnston* (New York: Knickerbocker Press, 1901), p. 218.

32. In his study of early Pittsburgh, Russell J. Ferguson states that "nearly all 'Revolutionary soldiers and officers' had a belligerent contempt for Alexander Hamilton's aristocratic 'Society of the Cincinnati' " (*Early Western Pennsylvania Polititcs* [Pittsburgh: University of Pittsburgh Press, 1938], p. 38).

33. Baltzell, *Philadelphia Gentlemen*, p. 141.

34. Ibid., p. 130.

35. Thorstein Veblen, *The Theory of the Leisure Class* (1931), as quoted by Reinhard Bendix and Seymour Martin Lipset in *Class, Status and Power: A Reader in Social Stratification* (Glencoe, Ill.: Free Press, 1953), p. 39.

36. Robert McKnight, "Diaries 1840–1842," Darlington Library, University of Pittsburgh. He was reputed to have had a million dollars before his wife received her share of the estate of her father, Harmer Denny, who left an estate of $16 to $20 million in 1852.

37. Nathaniel Burt, *First Families: The Making of an American Aristocracy* (Boston: Little, Brown, 1970), p. 6.

CHAPTER VI
Geographic Mobility

1. J. M. Riddle and M. M. Murray, *The Pittsburgh Directory for 1819* (Pittsburgh, 1819).

2. The United States Census for 1850 reported a population of 21,439 for these wards. Ten years later they had scarcely lost population (20,748 in 1860), but thereafter their population continued to decline: 13,378 in 1870, 13,116 in 1880, 12,658 in 1890, and 8,217 in 1900.

3. The Founding Families seemed to have a sentimental attachment to residence, especially "the old homestead." This was true of urban as well as rural homesteads. Hence some founding family members may have remained in a decaying area instead of moving to a more fashionable neighborhood.

4. The first "laws" of migration were advanced in 1885 by Ernest G. Ravenstein ("The Laws of Migration," *Journal of the Royal Statistical Society* 48, pt. 2 [June 1885]: 167–227, and 52 [June 1889]: 241–301, as quoted by Everett S. Lee, "A Theory of Migration," in *Population Geography: A Reader* ed. George J. Demko, Harold M.. Rose, and George A. Schnell [New York: McGraw-Hill, 1970], pp. 288–98). Ravenstein's theories of migration have been generally accepted by demographers, "the twentieth century having brought no comparable excursion to migration theory" (ibid., p. 289).

Donald J. Bogue makes a distinction among the various types of migration which will be noted in the case of the founding families. Changes of residence are divided into three major classes: moves within the same community, movement from one community to another, and international migration ("Internal migration," in *The Study of Population,* ed. Philip M. Hauser and Otis D. Duncan [Chicago: University of Chicago Press, 1959], pp. 486–509.

5. John W. Jordan, *Genealogical and Personal History of Beaver County, Pennsylvania* (New York: The Lewis Historical Publishing Co., 1914), vol. 1, p. 194.

CHAPTER VII
The Family

1. For an explanation of the upper-class family's peculiar social patterns in which its solidarity, tradition, and social status tend to assume a position of ascendance over the individual's interests, see Ruth S. Cavan, *The American Family,* 4th ed. (New York: Crowell, 1969), pp. 85–111.

2. This is not to deny the existence of social mobility, which, in varying rates, has always existed in American society. Indeed, marriage has often been used as an indicator of social mobility. While marriage can be a cause of vertical social mobility, it typically is an indicator of social mobility which has already taken place. In any case, it is not the intent here to judge the relationship between marriage and social mobility or to identify which is cause and which is effect.

August B. Hollingshead found that in the middle class, marriage tends to be a family affair only, whereas in the upper class, not only the family exercises control over mate selection, but the entire class is interested in the preservation of class lines. In New Haven, 59 percent of the females in the upper upper class selected husbands who were also in the upper upper class, 36 percent were from the lower upper class, and the remaining 5 percent were from the upper middle class; none were from below that class. Clearly, upper-class marriages tend to take place within that class or to an adjacent class ("Cultural Factors in the Selection of Marriage Mates," *American Sociological Review* 15 [October 1950]: 625–26). In Elmtown, even casual dating generally took place within the respective social classes (August B. Hollingshead, *Elmtown's Youth* [New York: Wiley, 1949], pp. 197–98).

3. Because Powelson's index has been proved a legitimate representation of Pittsburgh's old upper class and the twenty family sam-

ple was selected from it, it was appropriate to use the entire index in order to obtain statistical information of such quantity as to be statistically significant. Marriages within the twenty family sample did occur, but the frequency of such unions was too low to warrant a separate classification.

4. Edward Digby Baltzell, *Philadelphia Gentlemen: The Making of a National Upper Class* (New York: Free Press, 1958), pp. 17–30.

5. The Yule's Q equation is as follows:

	Core	Non-core
Successful	235	223
Declined	82	69

$$Q = \frac{ad-bc}{ad+bc} = \frac{16215-18286}{16215+18286} = \frac{-2071}{34501} = -0.06002$$

where the table is

a	b
c	d

6. Charles A. Beard and Mary R. Beard, *The Rise of American Civilization* (New York: Macmillan, 1937), vol. 2, p. 388.

7. Adelaide M. Nevin, *The Social Mirror: A Character Sketch of the Women of Pittsburgh and Vicinity During the First Century of the County's Existence* (Pittsburgh: T. W. Nevin, 1888), "society" section, p. 138.

8. In Elmtown, the average number of children per upper-class family was 1.5 compared to 5.6 for the lower lower-class family (Hollingshead, *Elmtown's Youth*, chap. 5).

9. The differences in family size between the core and non-core were small, especially in the 1820 and 1900 periods when the core group had slightly larger families. The small family became popular with the non-core earlier, 57 percent of that group having three children or less in the 1860 period as compared to 38 percent for the core.

10. Baltzell found that Philadelphians listed in both *Who's Who in America* and the *Social Register* in 1940 had more children than those listed only in *Who's Who in America*, 2.9 as compared to 2.8. Nothing is said about upper-class family size relative to the entire population, however. Baltzell, *Philadelphia Gentlemen*, pp. 160–61.

11. James H. S. Bossard and Eleanor S. Boll, *The Sociology of Child Development* (New York: Harper, 1966), pp. 274–75.

12. John McClure, family founder and son of an exceedingly

wealthy estate owner, did receive the manor house in addition to land. It is not known if he was the eldest son.

CHAPTER VIII
Social Institutions

1. Liston Pope, "Religion and the Class Structure," *Annals of the American Academy of Political and Social Science* 256 (March 1948): 89.

2. James Thayer Addison, *The Episcopal Church in the United States, 1789–1931* (New York: Scribner, 1951), pp. 65–73; Carl Bridenbaugh, *Cities in Revolt: Urban Life in America, 1743–1776* (New York: Oxford University Press, 1955), p. 152.

3. Mary Ann Gilfillan McBride, personal letter, 1846, Historical Society of Western Pennsylvania.

4. Margaret Gilfillan, *Alexander Gilfillan, 1746–1836; Martha Gilfillan, 1759–1840* (Pittsburgh, 1955), pp. 15–17.

5. Margaret Collins Denny Dixon and Elizabeth Denny Vann, *Denny Genealogy* (New York: National Historical Society, 1944), p. 189.

6. Benjamin Gifford Bakewell, *The Family Book of Bakewell, Page and Campbell* (Pittsburgh: William G. Johnston and Co., 1896), p. 73.

7. William G. Johnston, *Life and Reminiscences from Birth to Manhood of William G. Johnston* (New York: Knickerbocker Press, 1901), p. 264; Melvin G. Hollis and Peter D'A. Jones, eds., *Biographical Dictionary of American Mayors, 1820–1980* (Greenwood Press: Westport, Conn., 1981), p. 15. Barker received 1,787 votes to Guthrie's 1,584 (a third candidate received 1,034 votes). The governor of Pennsylvania pardoned Barker to allow him to serve as mayor. He made a poor mayor, however, and in the following mayoralty election (1851), Guthrie easily defeated him 1,911 to 924 (a third candidate received 1,206 votes). Mayor Guthrie was reelected in 1852, but lost his bid for a third term in 1853 (ibid., p. 145).

8. Gabriel Kolko, *Wealth and Power in America: An Analysis of Social Class and Income Distribution* (New York: Frederick A. Praeger, 1962), p. 129.

9. Dixon and Vann, *Denny Genealogy*, p. 182.

10. Gene R. Hawes, "The Colleges of America's Upper Class," *Saturday Review of Literature*, Nov. 16, 1963, pp. 68–71. Also see Edward Digby Baltzell, *Philadelphia Gentlemen: The Making of a National Upper Class* (New York: Free Press, 1958), pp. 319–20 on the increas-

ing importance and prestige of Harvard, Yale, and Princeton among the Philadelphia elite.

11. John N. Ingham discusses the relationship between the Pittsburgh iron and steel elite and Princeton University in the late nineteenth and early twentieth centuries (*The Iron Barons: A Social Analysis of an American Urban Elite, 1874–1965* [Westport, Conn.: Greenwood Press, 1978]).

12. Percy F. Smith, *Notable Men of Pittsburgh and Vicinity* (Pittsburgh: Pittsburgh Printing Co., 1901), p. 111.

13. "In these days of the national corporation and the national market, most gentlemen-businessmen of any stature belong to distinguished clubs in more than one city" (Baltzell, *Philadelphia Gentlemen*, pp. 340–41).

14. Oliver Ormsby Page, *A Short Account of the Family of Ormsby of Pittsburgh* (Albany, N.Y.: Munsell, 1892), p. 75.

15. George Wolff Fahnestock was an example of an individual committed to public betterment. He left the mercantile life, which he found a drudgery, to pursue his interests as a naturalist and an antiquarian. He was a member of the Academy of Natural Science and the Pennsylvania Horticultural Society, but also belonged to the American Sunday School Union and the executive board of the orphans' home at Gettysburg.

16. Felix R. Brunot, who had been captured by the Confederates, spent the war in relief efforts.

17. This accumulation of memberships was considered among the upper-upper of the eastern seaboard to be a sign of the nouveau riche or the uninitiated, who were impressed by quantity rather than quality. Belonging to the club at the top of the social hierarchy was more important than a long list of less prestigious memberships (Baltzell, *Philadelphia Gentlemen*, p. 356).

18. Liggett also belonged to the Pittsburgh Athletic Association, the Duquesne Club, the Pittsburgh Country Club, Sea View Golf Club, the Princeton Club of New York, the Ocean City Yacht Club, and the Ocean City Motor Boat Club. He was noted for his support of civic causes: he "cooperated to the utmost of his power in all movements which, in his judgment, tend to further civic betterment" (Jordan, *Encyclopedia of Pennsylvania Biography*, vol. 7, p. 105). In Liggett's case, this included his participation in Pittsburgh's Common Council and Select Council as well as his chairmanship of his local draft board.

BIBLIOGRAPHY
OF BIOGRAPHICAL SOURCES

The use of biographical encyclopedias and other compendia was essential to the gathering of basic biographical data other than that supplied by Powelson or individual family genealogies. In addition to the sources listed below, personal information was obtained from: city directories, the U.S. Census population schedules, newspaper obituaries, *Who Was Who* and *Who's Who in America* (both published on a continuing basis by the A. N. Marquis Company of Chicago), social registers, blue books, and church histories.

The Biographical Encyclopedia of Pennsylvania in the Nineteenth Century. Philadelphia: Galaxy Publishing, 1874.

Biographical Review, Volume 24, Containing Life Sketches of Leading Citizens of Pittsburg, Pennsylvania and the Vicinity. Boston: Biographical Review Publishing Co., 1897.

Blakely, Archibald, ed. *The Twentieth Century Bench and Bar of Pennsylvania.* 2 vol. Chicago: H. C. Cooper, Jr., Brother & Co., 1903.

Blanchard, Col. Charles, ed. *The Progressive Men of the Commonwealth of Pennsylvania.* 2 vols. Logansport, Indiana: A. W. Bower and Co., 1900.

Boucher, John Newton, ed. *A Century and a Half of Pittsburgh and Her People.* 4 vols. New York: The Lewis Historical Publishing Co., 1908.

Deacon, Charles R. *A Biographical Album of Prominent Pennsylvanians.* 3 vols. Philadelphia: Ferguson Brothers, 1888.

Encyclopedia of Contemporary Biography of Pennsylvania. 3 vols. New York: Atlantic Publishing and Engraving Co., 1889.

Encyclopedia of Genealogy and Biography of the State of Pennsylvania. 2 vols. New York: The Lewis Historical Publishing Co., 1904.

Fleming, George Thornton. *History of Pittsburgh and Environs.* 6 vols. New York: The American Historical Society, 1922.

Harper, Frank C. *Pittsburgh of Today: Its Resources and People.* 5 vols. New York: The American Historical Society, 1931.

History of Allegheny County Pennsylvanians. Chicago: A. Warner and Co., 1889.

Johnson, Allen. *Dictionary of American Biography.* 20 vols. New York: Charles Scribner's Sons, 1929.

Jordan, John W. *Colonial and Revolutionary Families of Pennsylvania.* 17 vols. New York: The Lewis Historical Publishing Co., 1911.

———. *Encyclopedia of Pennsylvania Biography.* 32 vols. New York: The Lewis Historical Publishing Co., 1914.

———. *Genealogical and Personal History of Western Pennsylvania.* 3 vols. New York: The Lewis Historical Publishing Co., 1915.

The Manufactories and Manufacturers of Pennsylvania of the Nineteenth Century. Philadelphia: Galaxy Publishing Co., 1875.

Memoirs of Allegheny County, Pennsylvania. 2 vols. Madison, Wis.: Northwestern Historical Association, 1904.

Moore, Alexander P., ed. *The Book of Prominent Pennsylvanians.* Pittsburgh: Leader Publishing Co., 1913.

Nevin, Adelaide M. *The Social Mirror: A Character Sketch of the Women of Pittsburgh and Vicinity During the First Century of the County's Existence.* Pittsburgh: T. W. Nevin, 1888.

Parke, John E. *Recollections of Seventy Years and Historical Gleanings of Allegheny, Pennsylvania.* Boston: Rand Avery and Co., 1886.

Prominent Bankers of Western Pennsylvania. Pittsburgh: Money and Commerce, 1915.

Rook, Charles A. *Western Pennsylvanians: A Work for Newspaper and Library Reference.* Pittsburgh: Western Pennsylvania Biographical Association, 1923.

Thurston, George H. *Allegheny County's Hundred Years.* Pittsburgh: A. A. Anderson and Son, 1888.

Williamson, Leland M. *Prominent and Progressive Pennsylvanians of the Nineteenth Century.* 3 vols. Philadelphia: The Record Publishing Co., 1898.

Wilson, Erasmus. *Standard History of Pittsburgh, Pennsylvania.* Chicago: H. R. Cornell and Co., 1898.

INDEX

Accumulation of advantages, 4–5, 118, 192, 209n3; and birth order, 162; and club membership, 181; and consciousness of upper class identity, 75; dissipation of, 100; and English immigrants, 39; and entry into the elite, 4; and family firms, 96–98; and family size, 163; and higher education, 194; and inheritance, 191; and maintenance of upper class status, 7; and marriage, 39, 152; and migration, 133–35, 139; and military service, 114; and national competition, 193; and occupational mobility, 77; and social mobility, 5, 6–8

Adams, Brooks, 91

Adams, Stephen Jarvis, 90

Age distribution of founding families, in 1820, 47–48

Allegheny City, 33, 46, 123, 125

Allegheny County: agriculture of, in 1820, 50–51; economic base of, in 1820, 48–55; family founders and upper class of, 11; history of, 22–24, 55–57; migration into, 58, 132–34; migration out of, 127–31, 134–39; population growth of, 46–48; and role of commerce in 1820, 48–50; as urban center, 43

Allegheny Observatory, 106

Allegheny River, 22

Amity Plantation, 36

Anderson, Col. James, 25

Anderson, Maj. William, 25

Anderson and Phillips, Iron Founders, 133

Anshutz, Alfred (1817–1890), 150

Anshutz, Charles W. (1840–1900), 97

Anshutz, Emma, 90

Anshutz, George (founder), 27, 28, 35, 133; career of, 25, 27, 88, 98; family participation in business of, 157

Anshutz, George, Jr. (1781–1852), 44, 98

Anshutz, Henry (1812–1887), 89, 133

Anshutz, Lewis A. (1863–1937), 82, 114–15

Anshutz, Margaretta, 150

Anshutz Company, 82

Anshutz family, 64, 118, 150

Appalachian Mountains and westward migration, 22

Associate Reformed Presbyterianism, 109, 170

Audubon, John James (1780–1851), 101, 105, 132

Bakewell, Allan C. (1847–1919), 114

Bakewell, Benjamin (founder), 59, 60, 88, 110; business career of, 25, 28, 33, 40; family participation in business of, 157; religious affiliation of, 69, 109

Bakewell, Benjamin G., 171

Bakewell, Charles M. (1867–1957), 116, 136, 138